Praise for Let's Split the Difference!

"As always, Susan has a way with making the complex practical and easy to use. This groundbreaking book is the first book to focus specifically on using the multiple models of the Interstrength® Method to see the differences and similarities of types that have only one letter difference. That one letter makes all the difference in the world. This is a major contribution to type practitioners everywhere."
—Linda V. Berens, Ph.D., CEO Unite Media Group, Inc., President, Interstrength Associates

"Susan has developed a comprehensive resource for all of us who work with Jung's personality theory. This book will be extremely valuable in helping individuals identify their "best-fit" type code from multiple perspectives."
—Bob Mc Alpine, CEO Type Resources

"This outstanding resource delivers what it promises—a clear and comprehensive guide for zeroing in on key differences between types."
—Eve Delunas, Ph.D. LMFT, Author, Survival Games Personalities Play

"Structured and applications-focused, genuine and meaningful, logical and theory-driven; and pragmatic and action-oriented, Susan Nash's Let's Split the Difference will help type practitioners be more effective and authentic in client contexts from the initial introduction of type concepts to the creation of an in-depth plan for type development and self-discovery. It will join Sally Carr's Finding the Fit as a go-to resource on facilitating the best-fit type process."
—Katherine W Hirsh, D.Phil. (INTP), Author of Introduction to Type® and Decision Making

"Another valuable resource from Susan Nash! Let's Split the Difference is a practical guide for type practitioners offering a comprehensive overview of type theory, temperament theory and Interaction Styles in an easy-to-read format. Susan shares insights gained from her vast experience with type to give us a step-by-step approach to helping clients find their 'best fit' type. She illustrates with clarity how to sort between types that are similar, providing a way for type practitioners to develop their facilitation skills."
—Mary McGuiness (ENFP), author of *You've Got Personality*

"Understanding what drives, motivates and stresses your reports, peers and superiors is an invaluable ability in the business world. It empowers you to anticipate conflict, avoid it where possible or face it head on feeling that you have a few secret weapons in your armory. Susan's book is a comprehensive guide to temperament, type, and function-attitudes that should sit on every manager's desk."
—Alison Drewell (ENTP), Director of Store Operations PUMA EEA.

Praise for Let's Split the Difference!

"This is a much needed book to support coaches and individuals in exploring the differences in type. Susan has pulled together the strands of the complementary lenses of type with great clarity, intelligence and insight, and created a practical workbook that will appeal to a range of styles. As a tool to support individual coaching or team effectiveness sessions in organisations, or to help clients find their best fit, this will be an invaluable source of information and learning."

—Debra Woods, Coach, Consultant and Facilitator, DWMC Ltd

"It fits! It works! It helps! Want to get underneath the skin of how business people work things out together? Get this book - it tells you how to clarify type in straightforward ways that are easy to put into a business context. It's a real resource for you."

—Andy Cole, Head of Talent Vue Entertainment

This book answers the questions that almost every Type Practitioner eventually ends up asking themselves, "What else can I do to help my client find their Type?" The practical lay out makes it easy to target the key information for each Typing challenge and the brilliant "questions for" sections help practitioners, and interested individuals, by offering insightful questions for differentiating between Types and then guides the reader as to what to look out for in the answers they receive. The introductory chapters frame the theories used in a clear and straightforward way, particularly around the "lenses", and set the scene solidly for the practical "workbook" style chapters that follow."

—Senior Training and Development Manager: Major UK Bank

LET'S SPLIT THE DIFFERENCE

YOUR GUIDE TO CLARIFYING THE DIFFERENCES BETWEEN SIMILAR TYPES

SUSAN NASH

First published in 2009 by
EM-Power (UK) Ltd.,
9 Westwood Road, Marlow
Bucks SL7 2AT
Tel: +44 (0) 1628 891481
Fax: +44 (0) 1628 471259

British Library Cataloguing in Publication Data
A catalogue record for this book is available from the British Library

Nash, Susan M.

Let's Split the Difference: Your Guide to Clarifying the Differences between Similar Types.

ISBN 978-0-9563279-0-1

FIRST EDITION

Note: The material contained in this book is set out in good faith for general guidance and no liability can be accepted for loss or expense incurred as a result of relying in particular circumstances on statements made in the book. The laws and regulations are complex and liable to change, and readers should check the current position with the relevant authorities before making personal arrangements.

Inspiring, informative books for thoughtful readers
wanting to make changes and realise their potential.

Other titles in the series include:

Dating, Mating and Relating
The complete guide to finding and keeping your ideal partner

Deliver Outstanding Customer Service
Gain and retain customers and stay ahead of the competition

Starting and Running a Successful Consultancy
How to build and market your own consulting business

Teamwork from the Inside Out Field Book
Exercises and Tools for Turning Team Performance Inside Out

Turning Team Performance Inside Out
Team Types and Temperament for High-Impact Results

Contents

CHAPTER 3

CHAPTER 4

CHAPTER 5

Forward

The spark for this book originated in a discussion in 2002 between myself and Phil Kerr, who publishes the Australian Psychological Type Review. We were discussing the challenges individuals faced in deciding their best-fit type. When individuals are reviewing their results from taking the Myers-Briggs Type Indicator (MBTI®), many people struggle with distinguishing between what are their innate preferences, and what behaviours they have learned.

I had been introduced to the model of temperament in 1992 by Linda Berens of Interstrength Associates (formerly Temperament Research Institute) in an MBTI® qualifying program. Temperament represents a separate, yet complementary, theory to type (originally described by David Keirsey and Marilyn Bates in Please Understand Me). This insight had proved invaluable to me in better understanding my core needs and how this integrated with my best-fit Type.

In my work within corporations, I had found that applying the model of temperament alongside type helped individuals differentiate more easily between innate and adapted style and therefore gave greater clarity to type choice.

In addition, I had been able to explore, in some depth, the cognitive processes (and their link to temperament) in writing (with Courtney Bolin) Turning Team Performance Inside Out and the Teamwork from the Inside Out Field Book.

Phil and I decided to undertake a series of articles comparing and contrasting similar types who had different temperaments, yet had three preferences the same.

During the time developing these articles, Linda Berens further refined her Interaction Styles Model, and I began to also use this framework with clients. Viewing behaviour through this model also provided further clarification on type choice.

When we completed the initial series of articles, it seemed that this could be repackaged to present a practical tool for type practitioners to work with clients.

Many thanks to Linda Berens for her amazing additions to the field of type knowledge and to Phil for allowing me to publish these articles within a broader framework. I owe a debt of gratitude to the thousands of clients I have worked with that have provided my reference source. Finally love and appreciation to the wonderful family who live with me while I explore and apply these models.

Enjoy this book which focuses on similar types with different temperaments. Look out for a follow on series of articles and a book describing types with the same temperament, although different Interaction Styles next!

Chapter 1

How to Use This Book

> "Best-fit type refers to the type pattern that fits you best. No one description or pattern will be a perfect match to all of who you are. Your personality is rich and complex, and a "type" or type pattern cannot adequately express all of that richness. Each of the sixteen types comes in a variety of "flavours," and best-fit type means that the themes and preferred processes of that type seem to fit you the best."
>
> Adapted from Linda V. Berens and Dario Nardi, *The 16 Personality Types: Descriptions for Self-Discovery* (Telos Publications, 1999)

So you think an individual with preferences for ISTP and an individual with preferences for INTP are similar? Or ISFJ and INFJ? After all, there's only one "letter" difference – think again!

This book Let's Split the Difference has been designed as a guide to help you, or your clients, select their best-fit type. When individuals are initially introduced to the concepts of psychological type, either by taking the Myers-Briggs Type Indicator (MBTI®) or by self discovery, there can often be confusion on at least one preference scale. This book is designed in a workbook format to help clients reduce confusion and identify their best-fit type.

It contains a description of the four lenses of type, in addition to comparisons for similar personality types. These original comparisons were published in the Australian Psychological Type Review and are reprinted with the publisher's permission.

WHO CAN THIS BOOK HELP?

This book is for:
- External coaches and trainers who are working with clients in assessing individual talents.
- Professional coaches or trainers working within organizations.
- Internal and external career counsellors who are working with individuals in selecting best-fit type.
- Any individual who is confused about their best-fit type.

HOW TO USE THIS BOOK

This is a hands-on workbook, and throughout it you will find the material organized into different categories designed to create a learning experience that is interactive, inspiring, informative, and clear.

The information categories include:

GAME PLAN

An overview of what you will achieve within each chapter.

FOUL!

To clear up a perception that may not be accurate.

TIMEOUT!

A clarification or side note containing useful information to build type knowledge. This may include definitions, statistics and facts.

SCORECARD

A series of questions to help you review outcomes from each section.

EXERCISES

Instructions for activities that can be used to try on material and put concepts to work. These actions are focused on developing knowledge of type. For each exercise there will be a section labelled Try It On! You can use this section to write down your ideas.

What's in this Book?

This book is comprised of five main sections:

Chapter One: How to Use this Book

- This sets the scene about:
  - » Who will benefit from using this book?
  - » How to use this book.
  - » What is in this book?

Chapter Two: The Myers Briggs Type Indicator (MBTI®)

- This describes:
  - » An overview of the four preferences
  - » A detailed review of the four preferences

Chapter Three: The Four Lenses of Type

- This describes the four lenses that can be used to clarify type:
  - » Function-Attitudes
  - » Hierarchy of Functions
  - » Temperament
  - » Berens Interaction Styles

Chapter Four: Type Comparisons for Introverts

- This section presents a series of comparison of two different Introverting types with different temperaments and only one preference different e.g. ISFJ and ISFP.
- This section has been written to be read as required for type clarification, not necessarily in sequence. Feel free to jump to the desired type comparison that is relevant for you or your client.
- Each description includes:
  - » The similarities between each pair
  - » The differences between the two types using the additional lenses of functions, temperament and Interaction Style
  - » Questions to help differentiate between the types
  - » An exercise to summarize the differences

- Each description has been written to provide an overview of the main commonalities and differences between similar types. More detail on the lenses of type is also included at the beginning of the book.
- In addition, the detailed type descriptions in the appendix may provide further insight to help identify best-fit type.
- Finally, as one book cannot capture the complete complexity of type information, there is a thorough Resource Guide in the Appendix which lists further reference sources for more in-depth knowledge and application.

Chapter Five: Type Comparisons for Extraverts
- This section presents a series of comparison of two different Extraverting types with different temperaments and only one preference different e.g. ESFJ and ESFP.
- Each description includes:
  - » The similarities between each pair
  - » The differences between the two types using the additional lenses of functions, temperament and Interaction Style
  - » Questions to help differentiate between the types
  - » An exercise to summarize the differences
- Each description has been written to provide an overview of the main commonalities and differences between similar types. More detail on the lenses of type is also included at the beginning of the book.
- In addition, the detailed type descriptions in the appendix may provide further insight to help identify best-fit type.
- Finally, as one book cannot capture the complete complexity of type information, there is a thorough Resource Guide in the Appendix which lists further reference sources for more in-depth knowledge and application.

WHAT ELSE?

Feel free to make the book your own: write in the spaces provided, complete the exercises and make a note of your learning. Remember, any behaviour change needs constant reinforcement: use this book as one of the tools in your toolkit in building type knowledge.

Chapter 2

The Myers-Briggs Type Indicator (MBTI®)

The Myers-Briggs Type Indicator® is a psychometric questionnaire designed to assess psychological preferences in the way individuals innately Perceive (or gather) data and Judge (or make) decisions. These preferences were extrapolated from the typological theories originated by Carl Gustav Jung in his book Psychological Types (1921).

GAME PLAN

In this section we will:

- Review the Myers Briggs Type Indicator (MBTI®) instrument
- Describe the four dichotomies in some detail

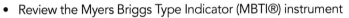

The study of psychological type was initiated by Carl Jung. Jung described how individuals innately access information and make decisions. He described four mental functions (or cognitive processes) that individuals might use to gather information, and four mental functions (or cognitive processes) that individuals might use to make decisions. We will describe these function-attitudes in some detail in Chapter Three.

The Myers Briggs Type Indicator (MBTI®) was designed to try to assess which of Jung's cognitive processes an individual uses most easily and then in what sequence they tend to naturally be accessed. It provides a four-letter code (e.g. ESTJ) which in essence, acts as a license plate to broadly describe how an individual might approach the world and the typical behaviours that he/she might demonstrate.

> **FOUL!**
> Too often people confuse Psychological type with the Myers-Briggs Type Indicator (MBTI). The MBTI is the assessment tool , Psychological type is the core theory. Do not confuse MBTI® with type!

THE FOUR PREFERENCES

The Myers-Briggs Type Indicator (MBTI®) attempts to assess preferences on four dichotomies as shown below:

Direction of Energy	
Extraverting (E)	**Introverting (I)**
In what direction does your energy naturally flow?	
If you have an Extraverting preference, energy naturally flows out first to the external world of people and events. More time is spent initiating and externally processing before internal reflection.	If you have an Introverting preference, energy naturally flows inward first to thoughts and reflections. More time is spent receiving and reflecting before external processing.
Perceiving Function (Gathering Data)	
Sensing (S)	**Intuiting (N)**
What type of information do you perceive from the world?	
If you have a Sensing preference, you tend to naturally attend most to information from your five senses; through what you see, hear, smell, touch, and feel. These observations can be in the moment or recalled from the past. Some who use the Sensing preference are incredibly aware of their immediate environment, while others can replay the sights, sounds and sensations of the past like a videotape.	If you have an iNtuiting preference, you naturally attend to information from concepts, ideas and inferred meaning. These observations can appear as the unrestrained exploration of ideas or as a total picture. Some who use the iNtuiting preference excel in seeing possibilities and reading between the lines, while others are able to manifest a complete vision, such as an "aha" or shower solution.

Judging Function (Making Decisions)	
Thinking (T)	Feeling (F)
What criteria do you use to make decisions or judgments?	
If you make decisions using a Thinking preference, you tend to prefer objective, logical criteria such as facts, data and principles. This can look like systematic sequencing and organization of logical data, or categorization of data and analysis of principles and models.	If you make decisions using a Feeling preference, you tend to prefer subjective criteria such as personal values or a harmonious result. This can look like an expressive demonstration of empathy and appropriate communication or tolerance of differences and an internal standard of fairness.
Function in External World	
Judging (J)	Perceiving (P)
How do you prefer to function in the external world?	
People with a Judging preference usually prefer closure and tend to push to make decisions. They tend to naturally make plans and structure outcomes.	People with a Perceiving preference either make decisions and change them easily, or postpone making a decision at all. They tend to be more spontaneous and flexible.

By selecting our innate preference from each of these four dichotomies above we end up with a four letter "code." Let's look at these preferences in more detail now.

Extraverting and Introverting

Many analysts of personality think of Extraverting and Introverting in terms of where you get your energy: from the outer world (Extraverting) or the inner world (Introverting) but this is not how Jung originally described the two terms. His description of the two terms is listed below:

TIMEOUT!
- Extraverting is defined as the process which occurs when your energy naturally first flows outward to the external world of people and events before moving inwards to the world of ideas and thoughts.
- Introverting is defined as the process which occurs when your energy naturally first flows to the world of ideas and thoughts before moving outwards to the world of people and events.

FOUL!
- We have to live in both worlds.
- Just because an individual has an Extraverting preference does not mean that they never reflect and allow their energy to move inwards.
- In the same way, just because an individual has an Introverting preference does not mean that they never come out to interact.
- The terms Extraverting and Introverting reflect where your energy flows FIRST most naturally.

The more detailed behaviours that TEND TO BE associated with Extraverting and Introverting are listed in the chart below:

FOUL!

As these behaviours come from preferences and not traits, you MAY see these signals.

The behaviours are situational and preferences influence but do not necessarily predict behaviour.

Extraverting (E)	Introverting (I)
Energy naturally flows outward	Energy flows inward to process and reflect
Act first, then think (initiate)	Think first, then act (respond)
Process information in the external world; talk everything over	Process information in the internal world; think everything over
Are easier to "read": Self-disclose readily	Are harder to "read": Share personal information with a few close people
May talk more than listen	May listen more than talk
May communicate with enthusiasm	May keep enthusiasm to self

Use more expressive body language	Use more reserved body language
Respond quickly; verbal stream of consciousness	Respond after taking the time to think; more deliberate speaking
Lots of diverse relationships	Smaller number of in-depth relationships
Seek outer world validation	Seek inner world validation

Sensing and iNtuiting

Jung identified two main ways that we tend to gather or perceive information: Sensing and iNtuiting.

TIMEOUT!

- Individuals who prefer the Sensing process, tend to primarily attend to information gathered through their senses such as sight, sound, smell, touch and taste. They tend to trust whatever can be measured or documented and what is real and concrete. They tend to use language which contains specific words and real-life examples.
- Individuals who prefer the iNtuiting process attend to information gathered through ideas, patterns, possibilities, hypotheses, and inferred meanings. They also tend to trust abstract concepts, ideas and potential, minimizing the importance of concrete evidence. They tend to use more abstract language which contains more general and metaphorical words.

2.1 More detail on concrete and abstract language is included in the Teamwork from the Inside Out Field Book Chapter Two.

The more detailed behaviours that MAY BE associated with a Sensing and iNtuiting orientation are listed in the chart below.

Sensing (S)	iNtuiting (N)
Tend to trust what is concrete—see, hear, touch, feel, taste, etc.	Tend to trust what is abstract—concepts, theories, etc.
May value realism and common sense	May value imagination and innovation
Trust what is measured and documented; rely on data	Trust theories and impressions
Like new ideas if they have practical application	Like new ideas and models for their own sake

May create new approaches from past experience and what is happening in the moment	May create new approaches from thoughts and hypotheses
Present information sequentially step-by-step or briefly and to the point	Present information organized around a conceptual framework or metaphor
Tend to be more practical	Tend to be more conceptual
Move from specific to general: start with the details and move to the end result	Move from general to specific: start with the end result and then build up the steps
Use concrete language	Use abstract language
Notice specific facets like changes in someone's appearance; can be frustrated when others are oblivious to the concrete environment	Notice and interpret what's between the lines in communication; can be frustrated when others take things literally
At their best are realistic but may at times appear too focused on the what they are observing or have experienced	At their best are visionary but may at times appear impractical

Thinking and Feeling

Jung identified two main ways that we tend to make decisions or judge events: Thinking and Feeling. Both are rational decision-making processes, they are simply based on different criteria.

TIMEOUT!
- Individuals who make decisions primarily based on a Thinking preference, tend to be more interested in objective criteria such as what is logical and what will service the bottom line. They may see criteria as black and white and want to make sure criteria are consistently applied.
- Individuals who make decisions primarily based on a Feeling preference, tend to be more interested in subjective criteria such as personal values and the people involved. They may see criteria as more like shades of gray and want to consider special circumstances.

Listed below are some of the characteristic behaviours that MAY BE associated with a Thinking and Feeling preference.

Thinking (T)	Feeling (F)
Use objective criteria	Use subjective criteria
Focus on facts, logic, truth and underlying principles	Focus on human values, needs, people and harmony
Analyze the problem without personalizing it	Consider the effect on others or what it means to them
Weigh the pros and cons objectively	Measure importance to self and others
Goal = justice and fairness, standards	Goal = harmony and integrity, see the exception to the rule
Tend to be task focused	Tend to be relationship focused
May appear critical	May appear illogical
Truth over tact	Tact over truth
Feelings are valid if logical: they need to be understood to be truly felt	Feelings are always valid: they are felt and difficult to explain
Conflict can be energizing	Conflict can be gut wrenching
Need to be in control of their emotions	Need to consider or express their emotions
Remember numbers and figures more easily	Remember faces and names more easily
Others say I sometimes appear cold insensitive, and uncaring	Others say I sometimes appear overemotional, illogical and weak

Judging and Perceiving

The final preference, the Judging and Perceiving Preference, was added to Jung's typology by Myers and Briggs to help to explain whether individuals used the Judging (Thinking/Feeling) or Perceiving (Sensing/iNtuiting) Function in the external world.

FOUL!
- Judging in this context means how we make decisions or bring our world to closure.
- This is not related to being judgemental!

TIMEOUT!
- Individuals with a Judging preference naturally use one of the Judging functions (Thinking or Feeling) in the external world. As a result they tend to prefer to achieve closure. They tend to make plans either by organizing resources to achieve an end goal, or by pushing for conclusion to achieve group harmony. Therefore individuals with a Judging preference tend to either like to have a structured plan or push for consensus.
- Individuals with a Perceiving preference naturally use one of the Perceiving functions (Sensing or iNtuiting) in the external world. As a result they tend to prefer to remain flexible. They tend to be open to possibilities either by exploring options from current concrete data, or by generating possibilities and reading future patterns. Therefore individuals with a Perceiving preference either make decisions and change them easily, or prefer to keep their options open as they explore new ideas.

Listed below are some of the characteristic behaviours that **MAY BE** associated with a Judging and Perceiving preference

Judging (J)	Perceiving (P)
More comfortable with a decision made	More comfortable leaving options open
Prefer to adhere to their decision	Prefer to change a decision if circumstances change
Set goals and push to achieve them on time	Change goals as information becomes available
Prefer knowing what to expect	Enjoy adapting to new situations
Derive satisfaction from finishing a project and marking the achievement	Derive satisfaction from starting a project and process involved
Deadlines are serious: time is finite	Deadlines are elastic: time is a renewable resource
Prefer working with structure	Prefer going with the flow

Tend to schedule time, plan and organize	Tend to be more spontaneous
Fixed milestones and process	Emergent process

EXERCISE 1: YOUR PREFERENCES
Looking at the descriptions for preferences:
- What did you most identify with? Extraverting or Introverting and Why?
- What did you most identify with? Sensing or iNtuiting and Why?
- What did you most identify with? Thinking or Feeling and Why?
- What did you most identify with? Judging or Perceiving and Why?

TRY IT ON!
Extraverting (E) or Introverting (I) and Why?

_____

_____

Sensing (S) or iNtuiting (N) and Why?

_____

_____

Thinking (T) or Feeling (F) and Why?

_____

_____

Judging (J) or Perceiving (P) and Why?

_____

_____

Based on this review your best-fit type is: _____

E or I   S or N   T or F   J or P

2.2 If you want to review a little more about this type, see the brief type descriptions in Appendix Two and the reference sources for other type descriptions.

SCORECARD
- What were your key learning points about the dichotomies assessed by the MBTI®?

Chapter 3

Focusing Multiple Lenses of Type

> We have found different lenses that are compatible with the four-letter code that derives from the MBTI® instrument. When we use these lenses together we have a much better chance of being accurate with best-fit type and also of providing our clients with more information than we could if we used the MBTI® instrument alone.
>
> Adapted from Linda V. Berens and Victoria Roberts in *Career Planning and Adult Development Network Journal*, Vol. 19

GAME PLAN

In this section we will:

- Set the Scene
- Describe the Cognitive Processes: the eight Jungian function-attitudes
- Describe the Hierarchy of Function-attitudes: the pattern for each function-attitude in the hierarchy
- Describe the Temperament Lens
- Describe the Interaction Style Lens
- Review other Developmental Factors that can affect type development

When most people discuss psychological type, they tend to refer to only the four-letter code originating from the assessment tool the Myers Briggs Type Indicator (MBTI®).

In fact there are two additional lenses associated with type originating from the theories of Carl Jung and two lenses that are associated with complementary, yet separate theories of personality. By viewing behaviour through these multiple lenses we obtain greater insight into type choice.

The lenses are:
- Functions - Attitudes
- Hierarchy of Functions
- Temperament
- Interaction Style

We will be reviewing these lenses briefly in the introduction, and then referring to them in more detail during the text.

Visual One: Lenses of Type

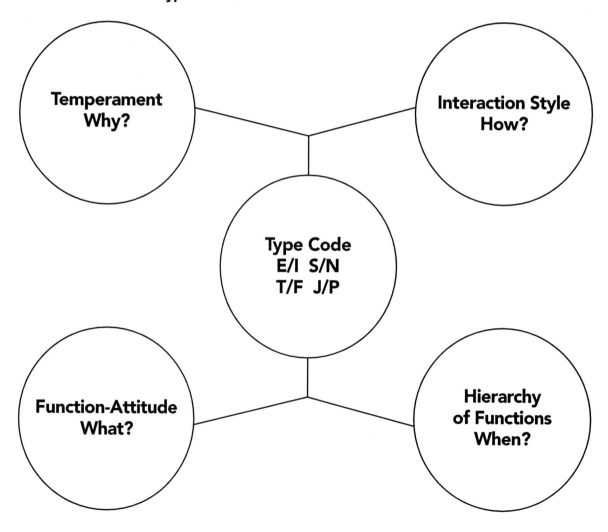

1. FUNCTION-ATTITUDES LENS

Katherine Briggs and Isabel Briggs Myers developed their assessment tool to try to obtain simpler access to Jung's theory of functions and attitudes. Unfortunately, over time, the MBTI® has often been substituted for Jung's original work.

Carl Jung's work covered an impressive array of subjects, but the theory that we will refer to for this book comes from his research and conclusions based around "typical habits of the mind" - similar patterns of behaviour that explained how individuals take in (perceive) information and make decisions (judge). The MBTI® is used as shorthand for the types of data different individuals gravitate toward and the varying criteria each person uses to make decisions.

TIMEOUT!
- Psychological type can be defined as an inbuilt pattern of information-gathering and decision-making processes.
- Type helps us to understand What data we perceive and What criteria we use to make sense of our world.
- Type represents the cognitive lens: how we think about things.

Cognitive Processes

Cognitive Processes are the specific ways in which individuals pay attention to and make decisions about information. Jung believed that our time is spent either gathering information (Perceiving) and/or making decisions (Judging). He defined the two Perceiving cognitive processes as Sensing and Intuiting and the two Judging cognitive processes as Thinking and Feeling.

There are two Function-Attitudes associated with each cognitive process:
- For Sensing: Extraverted Sensing (Se) and Introverted Sensing (Si)
- For Intuiting: Extraverted Intuiting (Ne) and Introverted Intuiting (Ni)
- For Thinking: Extraverted Thinking (Te) and Introverted Thinking (Ti)
- For Feeling: Extraverted Feeling (Fe) and Introverted Feeling (Fi)

For easier comprehension when working with clients, we defined one word to capture the essence of that function-attitude. No one word can capture the complete complexity of the process, however it can aid memory and practical application of the theory.

Information Gathering: Perceiving	Decision Making: Judging
Extraverted Sensing (Se) Experiencing	Extraverted Thinking (Te) Systematizing
Introverted Sensing (Si) Recalling	Introverted Thinking (Ti) Analyzing
Extraverted Intuiting (Ne) Brainstorming	Extraverted Feeling (Fe) Harmonizing
Introverted Intuiting (Ni) Visioning	Introverted Feeling (Fi) Valuing

Visual Two: Function-Attitudes

The following diagram depicts these relationships:

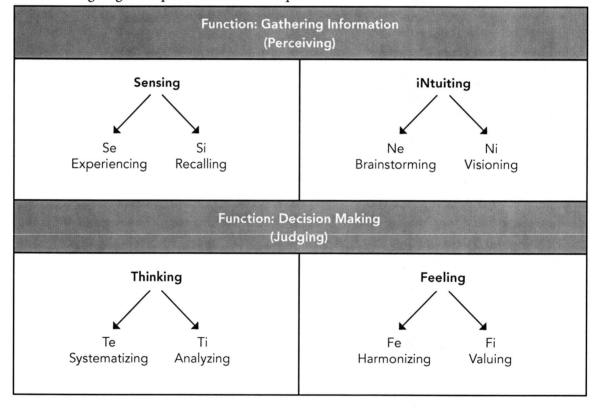

TIMEOUT!

- The way that each individual reacts to any given situation is often the result of a complex interaction between multiple function-attitudes.
- Rather like a pinball machine, an individual may bounce from using one function-attitude to another quickly depending on the situation and his/her comfort with each.

Information Gathering Function-Attitudes (Perceiving)

TIME OUT!

- Jung believed that we each have a preference for one function-attitude to gather information and one function-attitude to make decisions.
- He used the word preference to describe how a function-attitude is easier to use, takes less energy, is more natural and as a result, more consistently used.
- However, he also recognized that every individual potentially has access to all eight function-attitudes to a greater or lesser extent.

There are four ways of gathering information from which to make decisions. Every individual can use all four ways, however some are easier for us to use than others, take less conscious thought and require less energy.

Experiencing (Se): Extraverted Sensing	This function-attitude is defined as being drawn outward for the immediate, acute uptake and exploration of sensory data from the external world through senses such as sight, sound, touch, taste, and smell.
Recalling (Si): Introverted Sensing	This function-attitude is defined as pulling inward to recall past experiences and compare the present information to an historical data bank of stored sensory data and internal thoughts, feelings, sensations and memories.
Brainstorming (Ne): Extraverted Intuiting	This function-attitude is defined as being drawn to the outer world for the unrestrained exploration and interpretation of new ideas, patterns and possibilities that are not inherently obvious.
Visioning (Ni): Introverted Intuiting	This function-attitude is defined as pulling inward for the unconscious correlation of conceptual ideas, possibilities and symbols that enter consciousness as a whole system or idea.

Let's share below an overview of each information gathering function-attitude as it may appear when it is preferred.

Characteristics	Experiencing (Se) Extraverted Sensing	Recalling (Si) Introverted Sensing
Concrete or Abstract Language	Concrete	Concrete
Description	• Gathering concrete data in the here and now • Seeing options in the moment • Reading sight, sound, smell, taste and body language cues immediately	• Gathering sensory data and using it to compare and contrast with past sensory experiences • Past data can be viewed almost like a videotape • Know what's real
Time Orientation (credit to Interstrength Associates Facilitators Guide)	Present: What is here and now?	Past: What was?

Characteristics	Brainstorming (Ne) Extraverted iNtuiting	Visioning (Ni) Introverted iNtuiting
Concrete or Abstract Language	Abstract	Abstract
Description	• Implying patterns and meanings from current information • Reading between the lines to what is not obvious • Think out loud hypothesizing and exploring possibilities	• Data assimilated unconsciously comes into consciousness as a complete picture • Needs time to incubate before the idea is clear • Associated with "ahas" and shower solutions
Time Orientation (credit to Interstrength Associates Facilitator's Guide)	Unlimited: What could be?	Future: What will be

Characteristics	Experiencing (Se) Extraverted Sensing	Recalling (Si) Introverted Sensing
Work Signals	• Jumping into action • Reading and commenting on minute changes in body language	• Appearing more cautious as data is processed • Talk about what worked and didn't work in the past
Advantages at work	• Alert to small changes in the environment • Able to seize opportunities	• Protector of group memory • Prevent the reinvention of the wheel and repeating the same mistakes
Possible Challenges	• May jump in too quickly without the big picture • May constantly seek new sensory stimuli when bored	• May struggle when beginning new tasks or projects for which they have no experience • May appear negative as they talk about what cannot be done

Characteristics	Brainstorming (Ne) Extraverted iNtuiting	Visioning (Ni) Introverted iNtuiting
Work Signals	• Appearing positive and upbeat about possibilities • Constantly suggesting "What if? What if?"	• Appearing to step back before suggesting the total idea or solution • Will say things such as "I just know"
Advantages at work	• Stimulator of new ideas and possibilities • Energy can help achieve breakthroughs	• Initiator of innovative solutions • Able to simplify the complex
Possible Challenges	• May be reluctant to settle on one solution as multiple possibilities emerge • May seek continual change	• May be reluctant to accept other's viewpoints • Waiting for the solution to come to mind could delay projects

EXERCISE 2: YOUR INFORMATION GATHERING FUNCTION-ATTITUDES

Looking at the descriptions of the function-attitudes:
- Which information gathering function-attitude did you most identify with and Why? Experiencing (Se), Recalling (Si), Brainstorming (Ne), or Visioning (Ni)?
- Which information gathering function-attitude did you least identify with and Why? Experiencing (Se), Recalling (Si), Brainstorming (Ne), or Visioning (Ni)?

TRY IT ON!

Which information gathering function-attitude did you most identify with and why?

_____

_____

_____

_____

_____

Which information gathering function-attitude did you least identify with and why?

_____

_____

_____

_____

_____

Decision Making Function-Attitudes (Judging)

There are four ways of making decisions from the information gathered. Every individual can use all four ways, however some are easier for us to use than others, take less conscious thought and require less energy.

Systematizing (Te): Extraverted Thinking	This function-attitude is defined as making decisions using logical, objective criteria to structure the external world in the most efficient way to achieve the end goal. The output can appear as a structured plan.
Analyzing (Ti): Introverted Thinking	This function-attitude is defined as making decisions where the information gathered is categorized and evaluated against a model using internal logical criteria. The output can appear as a new frame of reference.
Harmonizing (Fe): Extraverted Feeling	This function-attitude is defined as making decisions using subjective criteria to optimize interpersonal harmony considering what is appropriate. The output can appear as a supportive environment.
Valuing (Fi): Introverted Feeling	This function-attitude is defined as making decisions based on subjective internal values and a belief system to validate individual differences. The output can appear as a fair and unbiased environment.

Characteristics	Systematizing (Te) Extraverted Thinking	Analyzing Ti Introverted Thinking
Objective or Subjective	Objective	Objective
Description	• Making decisions using logical criteria to sequence and organize resources to achieve goals in the external world • Using causal- effect logic	• Making decisions where information gathered is evaluated and sorted against an internal mental model • Analyzing data for what is logical
Work Signals	• Push for closure • Clear boundaries in actions: who is responsible for what and when	• Comfortable with gathering new data • Using questioning of ideas and data to clarify logic

Characteristics	Harmonizing (Fe) Extraverted Feeling	Valuing (Fi) Introverted Feeling
Objective or Subjective	Subjective	Subjective
Description	• Making decisions using subjective criteria to optimize interpersonal harmony and achieve consensus • Understanding what is appropriate in a situation	• Making decisions based on subjective values and an internal beliefs system to be tolerant of differences • Comprehending what is fair in a situation
Work Signals	• Push for closure • Demonstrate warmth and openness creating a safe inclusive environment	• Flexible and adaptable • Appear easy going and listen to and value diverse points of view

Characteristics	Systematizing (Te) Extraverted Thinking	Analyzing Ti Introverted Thinking
Advantages at work	• Organised and able to plan and prioritise work output • Assertive and to the point	• Able to disengage and ask questions to clarify logic in a given situation • Ability to repackage and reframe models and thoughts
Possible Challenges	• May push for closure too quickly and want to control too many decisions • May appear too rigid or blunt	• May be difficult to change their mind – "Not Invented Here" syndrome – want to win in debate • Internal decisions may be difficult to quantify
Aim is to	• Accomplish goals in a structured manner	• Improve a system or theory

Characteristics	Harmonizing (Fe) Extraverted Feeling	Valuing (Fi) Introverted Feeling
Advantages at work	• Able to recognise group dynamics & ensure all team members are involved in decisions • Build bridges between team members	• Act as the conscience of the group • Tolerant and supportive of individual differences – work well with all types
Possible Challenges	• May show all the emotions on face and in their body language: sudden outbursts of emotion • Find it hard to function when there is severe conflict present	• When values are crossed may appear stubborn • May lose enthusiasm for work when values are disappointed
Aim is to	• Make everyone comfortable and achieve consensus	• Achieve alignment between external world and internal beliefs

EXERCISE 3: YOUR DECISION MAKING FUNCTION-ATTITUDES
Looking at the descriptions of the function-attitudes:
• Which decision making function-attitude did you most identify with and Why?
Systematizing (Te), Analyzing (Ti), Harmonizing (Fe) or Valuing (Fi)?
• Which decision making function-attitude did you least identify with and Why? Systematizing (Te), Analyzing (Ti), Harmonizing (Fe) or Valuing (Fi)?

TRY IT ON!

Which decision making function-attitude did you most identify with and why?

_____

_____

_____

_____

_____

Which decision making function-attitude did you least identify with and why?

_____

_____

_____

_____

_____

3.1 If you want to learn more about Function-Attitudes please refer to the Resource Guide in the appendix.

The Hierarchy of Function-Attitudes: Conscious

The Hierarchy of function-attitudes provides an explanation of which cognitive processes each individual type tends to use, and to what degree of ease they are used. As all individuals can potentially access all eight function-attitudes, each type code is a short hand for the hierarchy of function-attitudes for that specific type.

TIME OUT!
- Each function-attitude can look a little different depending on where it fits in our hierarchy.
- Much of the work that has been done on the hierarchy of function-attitudes has been completed by John Beebe.
- He has developed a model of archetypes which show how the function-attitudes are expressed in an individual psyche.
- The function-attitudes are carried into consciousness on the back of the archetypes.
- Our top four function-attitudes tend to be more in our conscious control, the bottom four more unconscious.

Here is a brief description of the "flavour" that each function-attitude might have depending on its location. (For an overview of the hierarchy of function-attitudes for all 16 types, please go to Appendix Two.)

FOUL!
Please note that the words First, Second etc. do not indicate their strength, they simply describe the sequence in which you tend to naturally develop each of the top four function-attitudes.

Visual Three: The Hierarchy of Function-Attitudes: Conscious

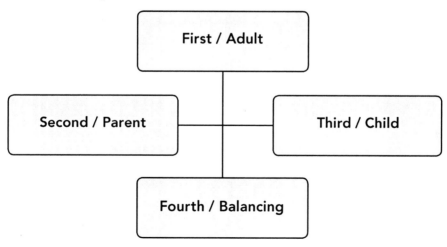

Conscious Function-Attitudes	
First Function (Adult) + Leading - Dominating	This is your most reliable, dependable and best-developed function-attitude. This is like your preferred hand: effortless to use, smooth, quick and easy. We also call this your Adult or Hero Function because it develops first and naturally comes to the forefront in a controlled manner. This is the function-attitude that we tend to lead with and with whose use we are the most effective.
Second Function- (Parent) + Supporting - Overprotective	This function-attitude is still relatively easy to access, but tends to develop a little later. It is not as consistently or reliably available as your Adult Function, but serves to support it. For instance, if your first function-attitude is a Perceiving process (Se, Si, Ne, Ni,) your second function-attitude will be a Judging process (Te, Ti, Fe, Fi) and vice versa. For this reason we call it the Parent function because it "looks after" the Adult function. For instance: an individual with preferences for ESTJ will use Systematizing (Te) as his/her Adult function to make rapid decisions, will rely on Recalling (Si) as a Parent function to ensure the decisions are grounded in reality.
Third Function (Child) + Relief - Unsettling	This function-attitude is generally more difficult to access when we are younger and somewhat inconsistent when used. We will call this your Child function because, when used, we tend to see a less developed, more playful manifestation of behaviour, which means that on a good day it appears fun and helps you reenergize, but on a bad day it can appear more awkward. When using this function-attitude there is a perception of highs and lows.
Fourth Function (Balancing) + Aspirational - Projective	This function-attitude plays a critical role in individual development. The Adult and Balancing functions can act as the "spine" of your personality. John Beebe named this the Axis of Integrity. If you develop a skilful use of this function-attitude, it can provide resilience and grounding to your behaviour. If this function-attitude does not develop, when you try to use it, it may appear "distorted" or "larger than life." A Fourth function appearing in stress mode appears more uncontrolled and "jagged." The Fourth function represents the link between your conscious personality and your shadow function-attitudes.

3.1 Adapted from John Beebe's type and archetype model: for more references on this model see the resource guide in the appendix.

TIME OUT
- The words under each function-attitude (originating from Linda Berens) provide brief descriptors for the positive and possible negative associations with each archetype.
- Each archetype can have both positive and negative influences on the personality.

3.2 If you want to review more about the archetypes and the one-word descriptors please refer to the Resource Guide in the appendix.

Visual Four: The Hierarchy of Function-Attitudes: Unconscious

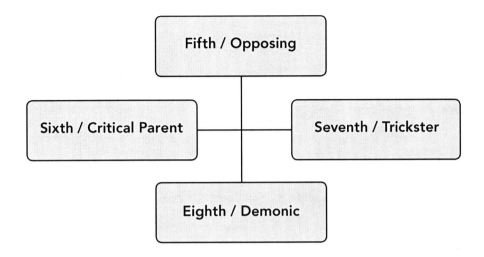

Conscious Function-Attitudes	
Fifth Function- (Opposing) - Opposing + Back up	This function-attitude provides the anchor to your shadow side. When you have to use this function-attitude, or it is "hooked" in some way, then we tend to use our four shadow side function-attitudes and appear unlike our normal self. This function-attitude can appear in an oppositional perspective: passive or aggressive. It speaks the same language as the adult but with the opposite approach. This is where we tend to demonstrate stubbornness. When developed this can provide depth to our Adult function.
Sixth Function- attitude (Critical Parent) - Critical parent + Discovery	This function-attitude tends to emerge under stress, and discourages and casts doubts. It can sound like a voice inside highlighting the negative. This voice can sound authoritarian and arbitrary. It criticizes, condemns, immobilizes and demoralizes. When developed this function-attitude can provide a profound sense of wisdom.
Seventh Function- (Trickster) - Deceiving + Comedic	This function-attitude plays the role of the rebellious mischievous child. The Trickster tends to put either you or another person in a double bind: two contradictory statements that have no positive resolution. If this function-attitude is developed it can help us overcome unreasonable obstacles and survive the Child function. It helps you get what you want in an untraditional way.

Eight Function (Demonic) - Devilish + Transformative	This function-attitude represents the most destructive and undermining aspects of our personality both to ourselves and to others. It tends to cause regrets later by creating confusion and disrupting trust. This can be the most rejected aspect of personality but the one that can bring enormous growth.

Hierarchy of Function-Attitudes: Summary

EXERCISE 4: YOUR HIERARCHY OF FUNCTION-ATTITUDES

- Map your hierarchy of function-attitudes (see appendix two for your type)
- Consider how each archetype might "colour" each function-attitude

Try It On!		
Function-Attitude	**Archetype**	**What this might mean to me**
Adult	• Easiest to use: auto focus/ home base • Things we know that we have not been taught • Capable of doing things in an outstanding way • Brings with it high energy • Have high ego if Adult function is strong • Have to "turn it down" to let others develop • We use this process to take care of our ambitions and goals.	

Function-Attitude	Archetype	What this might mean to me
Parent	• In Service Of - takes care of the Adult function • Guides the Adult in a non-obvious way • Supportive, shepherding, helpful and nurturing • Focus can be on the other person • More mature: stable parent figure • Dynamic is different for Introverts and Extraverts • Develops after the Adult function	
Child	• Brilliant but volatile: highs and lows • Divine child or wounded boy or girl • Self-nurturing or self-indulgent • Lightens up the personality: allows self to feel comfortable and valued • Less mature – never grows up • Delusional about abilities • Punctures pretensions in a light-hearted way	
Balancing	• Axis of integrity provides stability to the personality • Provides a bridge to the shadow side • Can have a sense of inferiority around the function: hence inferiority complex • Provides maturity, balance, passion and perseverance • Tends to ask questions • Can give energy and help us to get unstuck • Provides colour to the unconscious	

Try It On!		
Function-Attitude	**Archetype**	**What this might mean to me**
Opposing	• Anchor to shadow side • Appears in an oppositional perspective • Can be passive, aggressive, suspicious, seductive or avoidant • Starts from scarcity and fear • Speaks same language but with the opposite approach • How we get stubborn and argumentative • Provides defence of the self by challenging a point of view and seizing control	
Critical Parent	• Emerges under stress • Casts a spell: stops you from what you or others are doing • Can be authoritarian and arbitrary • Condemns, immobilizes and demoralizes • Discourages and casts doubts • Provides unhelpful criticisms of others • Puts a finger on weak spots	

Function-Attitude	Archetype	What this might mean to me
Trickster	• Rebellious, mischievous child • Puts you and others in a double bind: two contradictory messages provided when stuck in a situation • Springs the double bind but also helps you to get out of it • Trick or treat – Terrible Twos • Helps you get what you want in an untraditional way • Shape shifting – mercurial/paradoxical • Enables us to manage the child function	
Demonic	• Destructive and undermining aspects • Operates in the shadow to undermine ourselves and others • Pulls the rug out from others • Causes regrets later • Causes confusion and disrupts trust • Most rejected aspect of personality • Can bring enormous growth	

2. TEMPERAMENT LENS

TIMEOUT!
• Temperament can be defined as a pattern of needs, values, talents and behaviours that underlies our way of acting and being in the world.
• Temperament helps us to understand WHY we do what we do.
• The four temperaments are Improviser, Stabilizer, Theorist and Catalyst.

Four temperament patterns have been recognized and described for over 25 centuries and were popularized alongside psychological type by David Keirsey in his original book (written with Marilyn Bates), "Please Understand Me" and expanded for the 21st century by Linda Berens.

Temperament is a separate, yet complementary theory to type, which happens to relate to certain combinations of preferences. These four temperaments map onto the type code in the following way Improviser (SP), Stabilizer (SJ), Theorist (NT) and Catalyst (NF).

FOUL!
Temperament shows up in the type code by a combination of preferences but it is more than that. It is a separate theory that provides additional depth of perspective to type knowledge.

Each of us views the world through our own set of lenses distorting reality to match our own mental picture. We are all unique individuals with our own complexities and idiosyncrasies, but for 25 centuries four basic patterns have been consistently and cross-culturally recognized in the human personality.

Temperament theory is based on four sets of themes. People with the same temperament share the same core needs and values. This similarity does not mean that these people are all the same! There are wide varieties, but with strong shared needs. For example, string instruments are a family of musical instruments, but there are huge differences between a guitar and a double bass.

The four temperaments are listed below with their equivalents through history:

IMPROVISER (BERENS)	**STABILIZER (BERENS)**
Sanguine (Hippocrates)	Melancholic (Hippocrates)
Hedonic (Aristotle)	Proprietary (Aristotle)
Innovative (Adickes)	Traditional (Adickes)
Changeable/Salamander/Fire (Parcelsus)	Industrious/Gnome/Earth (Parcelsus)
Aesthetic (Spranger)	Economic (Spranger)
Eagle (North American Indians)	Mouse (North American Indians)
Mistaken goals: Revenge (Adler)	Mistaken goals: Service (Adler)
Dionysian (Keirsey/Bates)	Epimethean (Keirsey/Bates)
Sensing/Perceiving: SP (Myers)	Sensing/Judging: SJ (Myers)
Artisan (Keirsey)	Guardian (Keirsey)

THEORIST (BERENS)	**CATALYST (BERENS)**
Phlegmatic(Hippocrates)	Choleric (Hippocrates)
Dialectical (Aristotle)	Ethical (Aristotle)
Skeptical (Adickes)	Doctrinaire (Adickes)
Curious/Sylph/Air (Parcelsus)	Inspired/Nymph/Water (Parcelsus)
Theoretic (Spranger)	Religious (Spranger)]
Buffalo (North American Indians)	Bear (North American Indians)
Mistaken goals: Power (Adler)	Mistaken goals: Recognition (Adler)
Promethean (Keirsey/Bates)	Apollonian (Keirsey/Bates)
Intuiting/Thinking: NT (Myers)	Intuiting/Feeling: NF (Myers)
Rational (Keirsey)	Idealist (Keirsey)

* Adapted from information from Linda V. Berens Ph.D. and David Keirsey Ph.D. presented in Linda V. Berens Introduction to Temperament 3.0

A definition and overview of each temperament is provided on the following pages.

IMPROVISER	**STABILIZER**
Improvisers are driven by the need to live one day at a time, seizing the day and all the freedom they can get. They are opportunistic, act in the moment and want to see the immediate concrete tangible results of their actions. Improvisers gravitate to roles as crisis managers, problem solvers and performers. They enjoy work that is fast-paced and dynamic, with few "rules." With their present orientation, they possess acute sensory awareness and observation of physical clues (tactical intelligence), which enables them to respond quickly and tune into what other team members want.	Stabilizers are driven by the need to behave responsibly, wishing to serve and protect those that they care about. They are the pillars of society and need membership and belonging within a group. Stabilizers gravitate to roles where they are able to build and be part of a team. They enjoy a more structured formalized approach and want to contribute to concrete tangible outcomes. With their historic orientation they are able to translate learning from the past into current activities. Their ability to manage large amounts of sensory data (logistical intelligence) enables them to organize and institute repeatable processes.

THEORIST

Theorists are driven by the need to be knowledgeable and competent in all of their endeavours. They seek to understand the operating principles of the universe around them in order to create their own destiny. Theorists gravitate to roles that allow them autonomy and independence and call for use of their strategic visioning and critical thinking skills. They like designing and analyzing new abstract approaches to problems and systems. With their infinite time orientation and big picture thinking (strategic intelligence), they are able to provide clearly articulated frameworks and models to improve team performance.

CATALYST

Catalysts are driven by the need to be unique and develop potential in themselves and others. They are soul-searchers who are constantly on a quest for purpose and significance in their lives. Catalysts gravitate to roles that allow them to do something meaningful for this world and enable them to make a difference. They like roles where there is strong open communication and where they can achieve their quest. With their future time orientation and empathy, they are able to build bridges between disparate viewpoints (diplomatic intelligence), and create a cohesive team culture.

Characteristics	Improviser	Stabilizer
Estimated percentage of World Population	• Approximately 40%	• Approximately 40%
Driving Forces/ Core Needs	• Be noticed or make an impact • Get a result • Act swiftly and practically in the moment	• Be part of a group or team • Contribute to a concrete goal or accomplishment • Act responsibly and dutifully
Work Approach	• Seek to make a impact with their style and skills • Able to do tactical troubleshooting and fire fighting	• Get the right thing, to the right place, in the right quantity at the right price at the right time • Put in repeatable processes
Time Preference/ Focus	• The present: here and now	• The past: what was done before

Characteristics	Theorist	Catalyst
Estimated percentage of World Population	• Approximately 10%	• Approximately • 10%
Driving Forces/ Core Needs	• Be an expert • Retain autonomy and control in activities • Demonstrate knowledge and competence	• Be special • Have a greater purpose and meaning for actions • Develop their own and others potential
Work Approach	• Seek to improve systems and redesign processes Able to think logically and see strategic connections	• Build bridges between groups • Provide connection and enthusiasm
Time Preference/ Focus	• Infinite time orientation: scanning past, present and future	• The future: life is a journey forward

Characteristics	Improviser	Stabilizer
Thinking Style	• Contextual Thinking: reference all data to present context	• Sequential Thinking: Reference data step-by-step from start to finish
Communication Style	• Net it out/get to the point • Concise communication – less is more	• Linear and sequential: 1,1a, 1b, 2, 2a, 2a.1 etc. • Structured: beginning, middle end
Language	• Informal/casual with occasional slang • Creatively and humorously economical	• Respectful and appropriate to the group • Conventional
Humour	• Physical, tactile humour, e.g., Jim Carrey/Mike Myers	• Dry/tongue in cheek, e.g., Monica on Friends.
Relationships	• Fraternal: associated with buddies all on the same level	• Group bonding: associated with the family, team or interest

Characteristics	Theorist	Catalyst
Thinking Style	• Differential Thinking: where distinctions in points of view are seen first.	• Integrative Thinking: where similarities behind different data or points of view are naturally connected.
Communication Style	• Abstract around models • Critical questioning to examine a point of view	• Empathetic • Flowing and effusive
Language	• Precise and articulate • Avoids redundancy	• Generalizations and impressionistic • Employ hyperbole
Humour	• Play on words/cerebral humour, e.g., Steve Martin	• Self deprecating, often at their own expense, e.g., Bridget Jones
Relationships	• Expert: associated with any type of specialised knowledge or expertise	• Empathic: associated with genuine, authentic connections

Expanded and adapted from the Temperament Targets Linda V Berens : *Understanding Yourself and Others, An Introduction to the 4 Temperaments 3.0*

Temperament Lens: Stress

Another key benefit about understanding temperament is the insight that this might provide to us on our stress response.

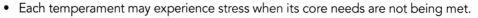

TIMEOUT!
- Each temperament may experience stress when its core needs are not being met.
- As a result, each temperament tends to react unconsciously in a certain way to try to get these core needs met.
- Eve Delunas developed a model to describe these unconscious responses or psychological games. (For more detail see *Survival Games Personalities Play* by Eve Delunas).
- These games can cause each temperament to react diametrically different from their core. The games in reality exacerbate the stress.
- The only way to regain balance is to find alternative ways, for each temperament, of getting their core needs met.

Improviser - Blackmail Game (Credit to Eve Delunas) Paradox: Move from Graceful to Disgraceful			
Purpose	**Triggers**	**Signals**	**Solutions**
• To get themselves excited • To get even with you	• Monotony/Boredom • Too many rules or no freedom • Not seeing concrete results - unable to make an impact • Want to show off something and feel good about it, but not getting the desired response • Experiencing redundancy and waiting	• Actively competes for attendion • Uses behaviour to get noticed • Leaves projects until the last minute • Doesn't do what they say they will do • Tells only part of the story • Stirs things up	• Find short-term success • Do something fun and exciting • Begin something creative, concrete and competitive • Give a new challenge • Provide "Cool tools" • Restore freedom • Reframe situations • Use more action and less talk • Stop all nagging and lectures

Stabilizer - Blame and Complain Game (Credit to Eve Delunas) Paradox: Move from Responsible to Irresponsible			
Purpose	**Triggers**	**Signals**	**Solutions**
• Excuse themselves so they don't have to be responsible • Entangle others	• Fear a loss of security or stability • Feel they can't say "no" • Feel like they are not needed/part of the team • Do not feel responsible • Believe there are challenges to their authority	• Announces all of the reasons why something won't work • Includes words full of "shoulds and ought tos" • Doesn't ask for help • Blames & complains • Internalizes self deprecatory judgments - may get sick • Gets worried and forecasts doom	• Give inclusion in new teams • Teach "I" messages • Redefine responsibilities – reduce overload • Provide security in other contexts • Teach them to be good to themselves • Identify concrete achievements • Encourage ownership of solution • Create opportunities for "play" • Teach relaxation skills

| Theorist - Robot Game (Credit to Eve Delunas) | | | |
| Paradox: Moves from Rational to Irrational | | | |
Purpose	Triggers	Signals	Solutions
• Preoccupy self • Distract others	• Perceive themselves to have failed in two or more areas • Viewed as incompetent by others • Fear they will fail again if they try to succeed • Fear about not being able to meet standards set by self • Having to work with others that are lower in expertise and competence	• Replays "perceived failures" over & over again • Does things to avoid failure rather than to be successful • Nit-picks - will obsess about making projects perfect • Engages in unnecessary debate • Takes up air time with pedantic, long winded paragraphs or can't find the right words • May intellectualize, use sarcasm, or dismiss others as illogical	• Reaffirmation of competence • New intellectual challenge • Refocus them into other areas • Give things to do they are good at • Consult with them in their areas of expertise • Stop all nagging and lectures • Give them maximum autonomy • Prescribe poor performance • Look for opportunities for success and mastery

| Catalyst - Masquerade Game (Credit to Eve Delunas) | | | |
| Paradox: Move from authentic to inauthentic | | | |
Purpose	Triggers	Signals	Solutions
• To alienate self • To deceive others	• No meaning in task/no purpose • Betrayal, phoniness, disappointment • Feel they have not been true to themselves • Pain of others • Loss of identity	• Disconnects from others (but not obvious) • Jumps from one topic to another - gets off course • Uses selective interpretation • Gets upset with little things and makes "biting comments" • Becomes inauthentic • Over-generalizes the situation and involves everyone in the persecution	• Look for a new cause or purpose • Obtain support from key people • Help them to be true to themselves • Frame as a growth experience • Present reality check to minimize generalizations • Provide reaf-firmation of uniqueness • Present genu-ine positive feedback • Encourage nurturing of self • Find and assert true identity

3. 3 Adapted from Eve Delunas *Survival Games Personalities Play*: for more references on this model see the Resource Guide in the Appendix.

FOUL!

- Remember the stress "game" is unconscious – you cannot tell the person "Oh you are playing the Blame and Complain Game."
- The only way to intervene successfully is to help an individual get their core needs met.

EXERCISE 5: YOUR TEMPERAMENT

- Which temperament do you most identify with and Why? Improviser, Stabilizer, Theorist or Catalyst?
- Which temperament do you least identify with and Why? Improviser, Stabilizer, Theorist or Catalyst?

TRY IT ON!

Which temperament do you most identify with and why? Improviser, Stabilizer, Theorist or Catalyst?

_____

_____

_____

_____

_____

Which temperament do you least identify with and Why? Improviser, Stabilizer, Theorist or Catalyst?

_____

_____

_____

_____

_____

Visual Five: Temperament through Functions to Type

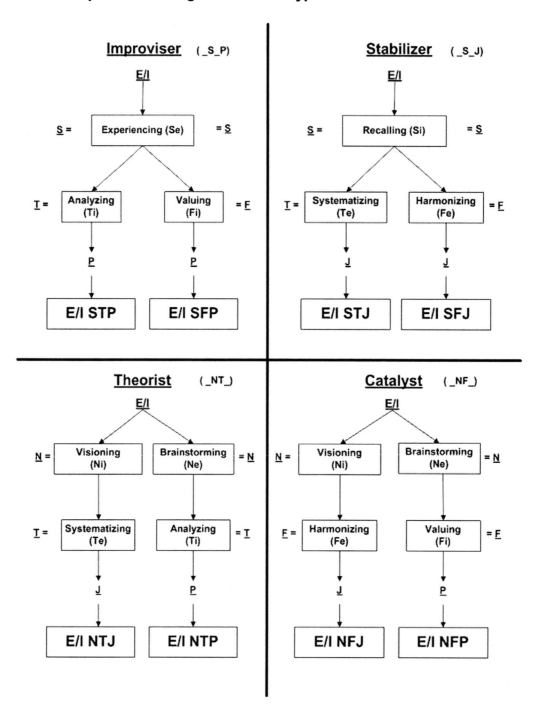

3. INTERACTION STYLE LENS

Another lens that can help in deciding best-fit type is the lens of Berens Interaction Style. Interaction Style is another SEPARATE yet complementary theory to type.

TIMEOUT!
- Berens Interaction Style has been defined by Linda Berens as an innate pattern of physical drives, mental aims and beliefs, talents and outward behaviours that underlie the ways in which we engage and interact with others to achieve our goals.
- Interaction Style helps us to understand **HOW** we prefer to relate to and persuade others.
- Interaction Style represents a psycho-physiological drive: the affective lens.

The concept of Interaction Style originates from William Marston's work on the emotional basis for our behaviour. Linda Berens defined these holistic frameworks as the four Interaction Styles and has linked this model to psychological type patterns. Each of us has an innate preference for one of four styles, although the style we use can be influenced by the context in which we are operating. Despite the fact that Interaction Style varies with the communication context, there is one of the four styles that we are naturally inclined to use.

The four styles have been called:
- In Charge
- Chart the Course
- Get Things Going
- Behind the Scenes

A definition and overview of the four Berens Interaction Styles is listed on the following pages.

In Charge	Chart the Course
• Like to move quickly towards a goal. • Believe that it is worth taking a risk to decide and correcting later. • Tend to appear quick moving, confident and determined. • Have a fast-paced tone of voice and energy. • Tend to naturally take action and lead a group to an objective. • Innately focus on executing tasks and removing obstacles. • Help to get things accomplished (often through people). • Are stressed by the appearance of nothing happening.	• Like to think ahead and predict the goal. • Believe that it is worth taking time to anticipate what might happen. • Tend to appear calm, intense and focused. • Have a measured tone of voice and energy. • Tend to naturally define the goal and then chart the key milestones required to reach the goal. • Innately focus on defining a sensible plan. • Help to keep projects and teams on track by comparing ideal achievement with current position. • Are stressed by not knowing what will happen.
FOUR VARIETIES (ONE PER TEMPERAMENT): • Executing actions as required in the current moment. (Improviser) • Making rapid decisions to organize and structure current reality. (Stabilizer) • Mobilizing resources to accomplish a clear future goal. (Theorist) • Mentor convincingly to achieve development goals for people. (Catalyst)	**FOUR VARIETIES (ONE PER TEMPERAMENT):** • Evaluating the most logical plan of attack based on the current reality. (Improviser) • Reviewing previous experience to create the most systematic plan. (Stabilizer) • Envisioning a future and creating a systematic plan to achieve the goal. (Theorist) • Having insights on future potential and working with an individual to develop talents. (Catalyst)

Get Things Going	Behind the Scenes
• Like to facilitate involvement from the group. • Believe that it is worth the time spent to engage others. • Tend to appear expressive, up beat and casual. • Have an enthusiastic tone of voice and energy. • Tend to naturally involve others in the decision to achieve buy-in. • Innately focus on motivating others and raising energy levels. • Help to raise commitment by focusing on exploring options. • Are stressed by not being involved or being left out.	• Like to invest in reconciling many inputs. • Believe that multiple points of view can be resolved. • Tend to appear approachable, friendly and patient. • Have a gentle tone of voice and energy. • Tend to naturally gather input from various sources and then repackage that data to a unique point of view • Innately focus on listening to others. • Help to avoid mistakes by gathering as much information and data on a subject as possible. • Are stressed by not having enough time or being given credit.
FOUR VARIETIES (ONE PER TEMPERAMENT): • Using playfulness to help others feel valued and involved. (Improviser) • Sequencing tasks to make life harmonious and easier. (Stabilizer) • Brainstorming possibilities to originate new models or points of view. (Theorist) • Imagining options to advocate a cause and help people develop. (Catalyst)	**FOUR VARIETIES (ONE PER TEMPERAMENT):** • Supporting those that they care about through actions. (Improviser) • Reviewing previous experience to support the team in the most realistic way. (Stabilizer) • Analyzing and integrating multiple models to define new concepts.(Theorist) • Valuing diversity and highlighting opportunities for developing others. (Catalyst)

Interaction Style	In Charge	Chart the Course
Aim	• Get an achievable result	• Get a desired result
Drive	• Urgent need to accomplish	• Pressing need to anticipate
Core Belief	• It's worth the risk to go ahead and act or decide	• It's worth the effort to think ahead and reach the goal
Decisions	• Quick and expedient	• Deliberated and purposeful
Energy	• Determined	• Focused
Style	• Social • Commanding • Confident • Driven & Straightforward	• Formal • Reserved • Intense • Calm & Composed
Want	• Control over resources	• Directed movement
Talents	• Lead to a goal • Execute actions • Provide resources • Mobilize resources	• See end result • Monitor progress • Devise a plan • Give guidance

Interaction Style	Get Things Going	Behind the Scenes
Aim	• Get an embraced result	• Get the best result possible
Drive	• Urgent need to involve	• Pressing need to integrate
Core Belief	• It's worth the energy to involve everyone and get them to want to	• It's worth the time to integrate and reconcile many inputs
Decisions	• Consensual and engaged	• Consultative and integrated
Energy	• Enthusiastic	• Receptive

Style	• Expressive • Energetic • Welcoming • Casual & Persuasive	• Gentle • Agreeable • Unassuming • Patient & Approachable
Want	• Expressed movement	• Control over quality
Talents	• Explore options • Share insights • Facilitate • Brainstorm ideas	• Support others • Reconcile inconsistencies • Encourage participation • Sustain efforts

Interaction Style	In Charge	Chart the Course
Preference in Communication	Both share **Directing Communication** which has an unconscious aim for focusing a discussion on a deadline. As a result, it can sound more like giving instructions, providing structure, telling and stating direction. The style tends to be more "stop-start" and can sound more staccato.	
Stressors	Out of control Nothing is being accomplished	Not knowing what is likely to happen Don't see progress
How to help	Tell them the reasons Help them see something is being done	Be calm and direct Let them know what to expect

Interaction Style	Get Things Going	Behind the Scenes
Preference in Communication	Both share **Informing Communication** which has an unconscious aim for engaging individuals in a discussion. As a result, it can sound more like making a statement, describing, suggesting and questioning. The style tends to be more "flowing" and can sound more open and eliciting.	
Stressors	Not being involved in what is going on Feel unliked or unaccepted	Not enough input or credit Pressed to decide too quickly
How to help	Listen as they talk things out Encourage their active participation	Be friendly but not too expressive Give time to reflect and integrate

3.4 Credit to Linda V. Berens: The Interaction Style arrows *Understanding Yourself and Others: A Introduction to Interaction Style 2.0.* For more information about Interaction Style, please refer to the resource Guide in the appendix.

EXERCISE 6: INTERACTION STYLE

Looking at the descriptions of the Interaction Style:

- Which Interaction Style do you most identify with and Why? In Charge, Chart the Course, Get Things Going or Behind the Scenes?
- Which Interaction Style do you least identify with and Why? In Charge, Chart the Course, Get Things Going or Behind the Scenes?

TRY IT ON!

Which Interaction Style do you most identify with and Why? In Charge, Chart the Course, Get Things Going or Behind the Scenes?

_____

_____

_____

_____

_____

_____

_____

Which Interaction Style do you least identify with and Why? In Charge, Chart the Course, Get Things Going or Behind the Scenes?

_____

_____

_____

_____

_____

_____

_____

Visual Six: Interaction Style Lens and Type

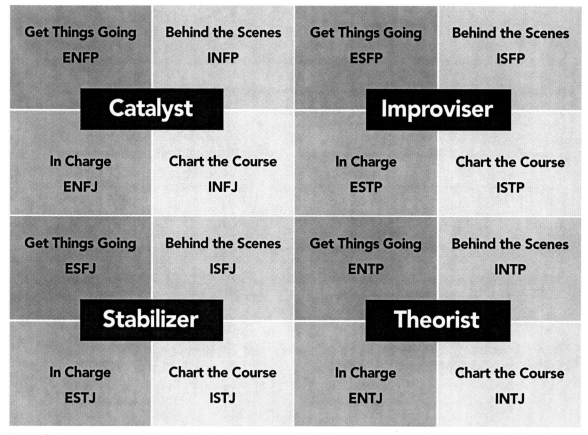

Get Things Going	Behind the Scenes	Get Things Going	Behind the Scenes
ENFP	INFP	ESFP	ISFP

Catalyst   **Improviser**

In Charge	Chart the Course	In Charge	Chart the Course
ENFJ	INFJ	ESTP	ISTP

Get Things Going	Behind the Scenes	Get Things Going	Behind the Scenes
ESFJ	ISFJ	ENTP	INTP

Stabilizer   **Theorist**

In Charge	Chart the Course	In Charge	Chart the Course
ESTJ	ISTJ	ENTJ	INTJ

Note: The temperaments and Interaction Styles are arranged in this way to match the Connects and Conflicts diagram from the Teamwork from the Inside Fieldbook Chapter Three & Visual 5.

4. OTHER DEVELOPMENTAL FACTORS LENS

TIMEOUT!
- While psychological type is inborn (Nature), many other factors can influence the development of our character (Nurture).
- Personality type preferences tend to be innate, however character develops as we interact with the environment.
- Rather like the ice berg, we only tend to observe initially adapted behaviours.
- As these might be specific to the personal or business context, it is important to self reflect in order to identify what are innate preferences and what is learned behaviour.

Many of these factors can cause confusion with individuals when they are trying to select best-fit type.

Factors that can influence our character development include:
- Work experience
- Age
- Upbringing/Family
- Education
- Culture
- Places you have lived/visited
- Intelligence

We use the **analogy of an iceberg**. We only see the tip of the iceberg: our adapted style for the context in which we are currently behaving. In reality, many of the influences of our behaviour are "under the surface." Some are part of "Nurture": our life experiences that have coloured our character. Some are innate and constitute our "Nature": our core personality preferences including temperament, Interaction Style and type.

Visual Seven: Iceberg

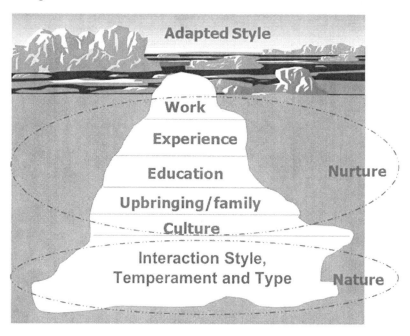

When trying to identify best-fit type, it is important to try to identify which is learned behaviour and which is adapted style. For instance, an individual identified best-fit type as ISFJ. Yet, she described herself as also being highly analytical and using critical questions, which sounded a little more like the Theorist temperament. On further discussion, she recognized that she had been brought up in a family of academics, and debate over the dinner table was expected! She realized that this was a learned behaviour rather than a preference related to temperament. In addition, her Child function was Analyzing (Ti) and this upbringing had hastened the development of this function.

EXERCISE 7: OTHER DEVELOPMENTAL FACTORS LENS

Thinking of your personality type:
- Which factors may have influenced your character development?
- How might they align with your best-fit type?
- How might these developmental factors have influenced additional talents that might not be associated with your best-fit type?

TRY IT ON!

My type is: _____

Factors that have influenced my character development could be...

_____

_____

_____

_____

They align with the talents of my best-fit type in the following way...

_____

_____

_____

_____

They may have developed additional talents in the following way...

_____

_____

_____

_____

3.5 for more references on development factors please see the Resource Guide in the Appendix.

SUMMARY

SCORECARD

- What were your key learning points about function-attitudes?
- What did you learn about the hierarchy of function-attitudes for your type?
- What did you learn about temperament? How could this help you in clarifying best-fit type?
- What did you learn about Interaction Style? How could this help you in clarifying best-fit type?
- How could developmental factors influence best-fit type?

Chapter 4

Comparing Introverting Type Pairs

GAME PLAN

In this section we will:

- Set the Scene
- Review pairs of Introverting types as described below
- For each pair we will:
  - » Provide an overview of similarities
  - » Discuss differences in temperament, function-attitudes and Interaction Style (if relevant)
  - » Provide questions to help differentiate between two types
- Discuss key learning points

FOUL!

Remember as you read the descriptions, different types may demonstrate similar behaviours for different reasons. Always probe for Why an individual is acting in a specific way!

For instance, if you observe that an individual is really organized, if you ask, "Why?" you might receive the following answers:

- "It makes life easier." (could be Improviser – SP)
- "It helps to create a consistent process." (could be Stabilizer – SJ)
- "It helps me to appear competent." (could be Theorist – NT)
- "It helps me to achieve the purpose." (could be Catalyst – NT)
- "I have learned to do this at school." (could be adapted behaviour)

SET THE SCENE

This section has not been written to be read in sequence. Rather it has been written to reference as required depending on the person and the similar types that they are trying to understand more fully.

Each comparison of pairs has been written as a summary of key similarities and differences between the pairs of types listed below. Feel free to reference the introductory information at the beginning of the book, the type descriptions at the end of the book and the Resource Guide for further clarification on potential similarities and differences.

Good luck in your sorting process!

	ISTJ	INTJ	ISFJ	INFJ	ISTP	INTP	ISFP
INTJ	1						
ISFJ							
INFJ		3	4				
ISTP	2						
INTP						6	
ISFP			5				
INFP						7	8

1. DISTINGUISHING ISTJ FROM INTJ

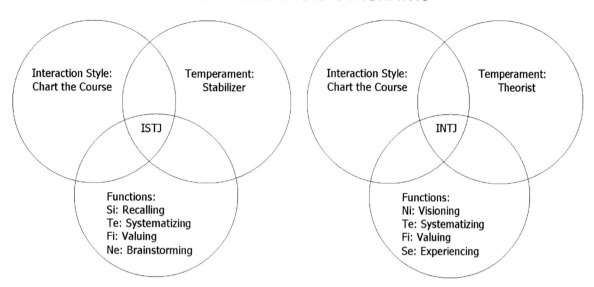

ISTJs and INTJs share certain **core similarities**. With an **Introverting** preference, using their first function in the internal world, they will both tend to be reflective, deliberate and thoughtful. Both types have the same Auxiliary/Parent function, **Systematizing (Te)**. This function-attitude leads to making objective decisions using causal-effect logic. Therefore both types can establish clear boundaries of "right" and "wrong", are organized and methodical. Both types use Valuing as their Child function so when a value is engaged, they may get hooked with childlike enthusiasm and excitement. They therefore can be loyal to a fault and may become easily hurt and feel rejected because of this vulnerable loyalty. Both types use the **Chart the Course** Interaction Style. The core drive for Chart the Course is to anticipate the goal and think through the actions to achieve this desired result. The Chart the Course style appears as intense, focused and composed. Both types tend to respond in relationships allowing the other person to make the first move. In addition the Chart the Course Style tends to use more directing language, with a time and task focus, by being clear about outcomes, providing advice or structure, and giving instructions. Both types share the **Judging** preference and, as a result, tend to view time as a finite resource, push for closure in the external world and stick to their plan.

However, there are also a number of **marked differences** between ISTJs and INTJs:

ISTJ	INTJ
Temperament	
ISTJs have a **Stabilizer** temperament. They need to know their responsibilities, and then demonstrate living up to these demands. Stabilizers value security, stability and are economical with resources. They innately institute structure into chaos and create repeatable processes. They enjoy contributing to team results yet value their own space.	INTJs have a **Theorist** temperament. They need to be knowledgeable and demonstrate competence in whatever ventures they deem important. Theorists value autonomy and independence in their activities. They employ intellectual rigour in their approach to facts and data. They view the world from a strategic perspective, with a constant eye to the future.
Stress Response Each stress response can cause the temperament to act diametrically differently from their innate abilities.	
Stabilizers (ISTJ) may blame and complain when they are overloaded and others have not lived up to their responsibilities. The paradox of this stress response is to move from responsible to irresponsible.	**Theorists (INTJ)** may become mentally paralyzed when they perceive themselves to have been incompetent. The paradox of this stress response is to move from rational to irrational.

ISTJ	INTJ
Temperament	
ISTJs, with a **Stabilizer** temperament, tend to gravitate towards organized and structured environments with clear accountabilities and hierarchy. Their relationships tend to be based around groups such as family, clubs, teams, etc.	**INTJs** with a **Theorist** temperament, tend to gravitate towards environments which are innovative and intellectual and allow them to demonstrate their expertise. Their relationships tend to be based around respect for competence in any field in which they are interested.

General Observations	
ISTJs enjoy thinking about and discussing concrete reality and data. They employ **sequential, specific language** which tends to layout practical information in a step-by-step manner, with lots of examples often referring to past projects. In addition, their thorough communication style is excellent when providing instructions, designing a process or establishing a plan.	INTJs enjoy thinking about and discussing hypothesis, models, theories and concepts. They employ **precise language** and will often correct word choice to ensure that their understanding of the information is correct. In addition, their enjoyment of debate, and ability to critically question the message in order to ensure multiple perspectives are considered, can help to dissect and clarify a point of view.

ISTJ	INTJ
Information Gathering Function-Attitudes	
ISTJs use **Recalling (Si)**. They perceive the current context, and then are able to refer back to their reference bank of stored sensory images. From this data they compare and contrast the current data with previous experience. As such, they tend to be able to bring the best of the past to the future, enable others to learn from mistakes and can provide the "group memory."	INTJs use **Visioning (Ni)**. They gather data from a variety of sources and then need to step back to allow the information to incubate. After this time delay, the complete solution/idea appears, and it can appear very different from the original facts. As such, they tend to be able to simplify the complex, come up with a unique future picture and unify different approaches.
As **ISTJs** mature and develop their Balancing function, **Brainstorming (Ne)**, they may demonstrate increased interest and passion in models and possibilities.	As **INTJs** mature and develop their Balancing function, **Experiencing (Se)**, they may develop new sensory hobbies such as painting, cooking, etc.

QUESTIONS FOR SORTING BETWEEN STABILIZER AND THEORIST TEMPERAMENTS

What drives you? What do you really enjoy doing?
- Listen for the **Stabilizer's (ISTJ)** drive for team membership, producing tangible results, and being responsible.
- Listen for the **Theorist's (INTJ)** drive for competence, autonomy, and being an expert.

What do you really struggle with? When was a time that you felt you had failed?

- Listen for **Stabilizers (ISTJ)** to describe projects with constant change, no meaningful role, no structure and no team support.
- Listen for **Theorists (INTJ)** to describe situations when they perceived themselves to be incompetent on two or more fronts, had no ability to influence future outcomes, were overloaded with details, or had no conceptual big picture.

QUESTIONS FOR CLARIFYING TEMPERAMENT VIA IMPROVEMENT OR REDESIGN

Is your drive to improve a system paramount and do you often search for a completely innovative system to accomplish the goal?

- If **Yes,** consider **INTJ,** because Theorists employ double-loop problem solving: they will look outside the current system to find an innovative approach.
- If **No,** consider **ISTJ,** because Stabilizers like to improve within the current context in order to increase efficiency or productivity and will only reluctantly discard the current structure.

QUESTIONS FOR CLARIFYING TEMPERAMENT VIA PRAGMATISM OR COLLABORATION

How important is it to do what is necessary to achieve the goal, even if your colleagues are not necessarily on the same page?

- If it is Important, consider **INTJ,** because **Theorists** tend to be more pragmatic at doing what it takes to achieve the goal.
- If the Team has precedent, consider **ISTJ,** because, even though individuals with preferences for ISTJ can appear more solitary, **Stabilizers** will still experience a need to contribute to and involve the team.

QUESTIONS FOR SORTING BETWEEN RECALLING (SI) AND VISIONING (NI) FUNCTION-ATTITUDES

When you begin a project, do you automatically think back to what you did before, and what worked?

- If **Yes,** consider **ISTJ,** because **Stabilizers** using **Recalling (Si)** tend to begin with historic data, and as a result are able to articulate what is real and practical.
- If **No,** consider **INTJ,** because **Theorists** using **Visioning (Ni)** may be unable to access past experience, as their energy is more focused on future models and plans.

1. Distinguishing ISTJ from INTJ: Review

EXERCISE 8: DISTINGUISHING BETWEEN ISTJ AND INTJ

Thinking of these two personality types:

- Which temperament seems like the best fit and why? Stabilizer (ISTJ) or Theorist (INTJ)?
- Which information gathering function-attitude appears the best fit? Recalling (Si) or Visioning (Ni)?
- What developmental factors might be relevant in selecting best-fit type?

TRY IT ON!

DISTINGUISHING BETWEEN ISTJ AND INTJ

Which temperament seems like the best fit and why? Stabilizer (ISTJ) or Theorist (INTJ)?

_____

_____

_____

Which information gathering function-attitude appears the best fit and why? Recalling (Si) or Visioning (Ni)?

_____

_____

_____

What developmental factors might be relevant in selecting best-fit type?

_____

_____

_____

2. DISTINGUISHING ISTP FROM ISTJ

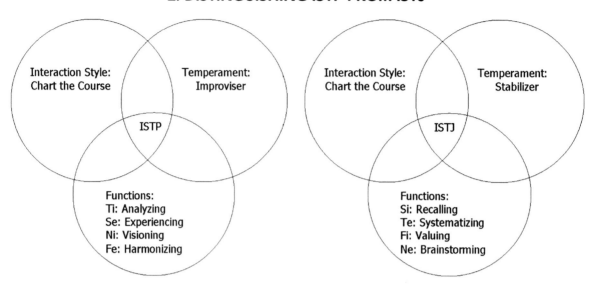

ISTPs and **ISTJs** share certain **core similarities.** Both types have an **Introverting** preference which means that their energy goes inwards first and they tend to reflect before speaking. This means that you may not observe expressive body language. Also, when interacting with others, they will often wait for others to initiate the conversation. They both use the **Chart the Course** Interaction Style, which means that they tend to naturally define the goal and then chart the key milestones required to reach the goal. They tend to appear reserved and private as they make deliberate, focused decisions. They are both directing in their communication style; comfortable providing specific instructions with deadlines and task assignments. Both share a **Sensing** preference which means that they tend to use concrete language, providing specifics, examples and stories as they interact with others. They enjoy dealing with physical facts, data and information. In addition, they both share the **Thinking** preference which means that they tend to make logical decisions using quantitative data and may be uncomfortable with displays of emotion. They are both practical, hands-on and focused towards achieving tangible goals.

However, despite these similarities there are also a number of **marked differences** between **ISTPs** and **ISTJs.** The following table will highlight a few of these key indicators.

ISTP	ISTJ
Temperament	
ISTPs have an **Improviser** temperament. Improvisers need freedom, like to enjoy the here and now and are driven to be impressive. They tend to innately make the most of any situation and are talented at seizing current opportunities. Improvisers tend to read individuals well because they innately recognize the motive of the other person: what they want from the situation. Improvisers value stimulation, variety and performing with skill.	**ISTJs** have a **Stabilizer** temperament. Stabilizers need to know their responsibilities, enjoy living up to these demands and are driven to follow through. They tend to innately institute structure into chaos and are talented at creating repeatable processes. Stabilizers tend to enjoy contributing to team results yet still value their own space. Stabilizers value security, stability and are economical with resources.
Stress Response Each stress response can cause the temperament to act diametrically differently from their innate abilities.	
Improvisers (ISTP) may escalate the situation and take action to cause a reaction. The paradox of this stress response is to move from graceful to disgraceful.	**Stabilizers (ISTJ)** may nag, worry and get depressed when they are overloaded and others have not lived up to their responsibilities. The paradox of this stress response is to move from responsible to irresponsible.
ISTP	ISTJ
Information Gathering Function-Attitudes	
ISTPs use primarily **Experiencing (Se)**. They read all the concrete data in the moment – sound, sight, smell, taste, and touch. Using Experiencing (Se) in this way, will often mean they will pick up minute changes in facial expression, movements in body language, and comment on them. They are gifted at making ideas concrete and real, and seeing options in the moment.	**ISTJs** use primarily **Recalling (Si)**. They perceive the current context, and then are able to refer back to their reference bank of stored sensory images, in order to compare and contrast the current data with previous experience. Using Recalling (Si) in this way, they will be able to bring the best of the past to the future, enable others to learn from mistakes, and can provide the "group memory."

Decision Making Function-Attitudes	
ISTPs primarily use **Analyzing (Ti)** to make decisions. This means that they are driven to dissect and categorize data, evaluating it against internal criteria, and make independent decisions using this mental model. Those who use Analyzing (Ti) with ease excel at examining an argument, creating a unique point of view, and approaching problems from various logical perspectives.	ISTJs primarily use **Systematizing (Te)** to make decisions. This means that they use causal-effect logic, "If this, then that" in the external world. Those who use Systematizing (Te) with ease excel at establishing clear boundaries of "right" and "wrong", tend to be organized and methodical, and excel in planning the most efficient steps and responsibilities to achieve the end goal.

General Observations	
ISTP's Adult function is **Analyzing (Ti)** which means that they make decisions internally but gather information externally and as a result appear more flexible.	ISTJ's Adult function is **Recalling (Si)**, which means they gather information internally and make decisions externally and as a result appear more fixed in their approach.

Thinking Style (credit to Linda Berens)	
ISTPs use **Contextual Thinking** which means that they tend to reference everything to the present context. This allows them to see what is relevant and when something is awry.	ISTJs use **Sequential Thinking** which means that they tend to reference data step-by-step from start to finish. This allows them to provide clear direction and see where something fits in a process.

Orientation to External World	
ISTPs have a **Perceiving** Preference which means they tend to be more comfortable with ambiguity and changing their decisions once they are made.	ISTJs have a **Judging** Preference which means they tend to be more comfortable with closure, and like to stick to decisions once they are made.

QUESTIONS FOR SORTING BETWEEN IMPROVISER AND STABILIZER TEMPERAMENTS

What drives you? What do you really enjoy doing? What was your best job?

- Listen for **Improviser's (ISTP)** drive for freedom, fun and seeing results in the moment, making an impact and being noticed.
- Listen for **Stabilizer's (ISTJ)** drive for structure, dedication and contribution to the team and being loyal.

What do you really struggle with? When was a time that you felt you had failed?

- Listen for **Improvisers (ISTP)** to describe long-term projects, with no tangible outcome, too many rules, and pointless details.
- Listen for **Stabilizers (ISTJ)** to describe pointless, constant change with others not following processes and procedures, and an inability to deliver on their responsibilities.

QUESTIONS TO CLARIFY TEMPERAMENT VIA CURRENT IMPACT OR PAST FOCUS

Do you need to see immediate concrete results from your efforts?

- If **Yes** consider **ISTP** because **Improvisers** tend to drive toward immediate tangible results. ISTPs may also talk about getting an "aha" (Visioning Ni as a Third/Child function) and then making it happen (supporting Experiencing Se as the Parent).
- If **No** consider **ISTJ** because **Stabilizers** tend to want to see tangible outcomes but in the proper time frame with the correct structure. As ISTJs mature they may also become more flexible as they access their Fourth/Balancing function Brainstorming (Ne) and seek possibilities before closure.

QUESTIONS TO IDENTIFY RULES VERSUS EXPEDIENCY

Do you prefer to follow rules and processes?

- If **Yes** consider **Stabilizer (ISTJ)** because Stabilizers innately respect the process and hierarchy as they follow approved guidelines.
- If **No** consider **Improviser (ISTP)** because Improvisers innately look for the easiest and most expedient approach to a situation (whether this is in alignment with the rules or not!)

QUESTIONS TO IDENTIFY RECALLING (SI) VERSUS EXPERIENCING (SE)

Do you tend to refer back to what was done before when starting a new project?

- If **Yes** consider **Stabilizer (ISTJ)** because Stabilizers using **Recalling (Si)** tend to go back to the past, evaluate what worked and what didn't work, as a framework to begin current plans.
- If **No** consider **Improviser (ISTP)** because Improvisers using **Experiencing (Se)** will tend to focus on the immediate concrete reality as they decide the next best steps.

2. Distinguishing ISTP from ISTJ: Review

EXERCISE 9: DISTINGUISHING BETWEEN ISTP AND ISTJ
Thinking of these two personality types:
- Which temperament seems like the best fit and why? Improviser (ISTP) or Stabilizer (ISTJ)?
- Which information gathering function-attitude appears the best fit? Experiencing (Se) or Recalling (Si)?
- Which decision making function-attitude appears the best fit? Analyzing(Ti) or Systematizing (Te)?
- What developmental factors might be relevant in selecting best-fit type?

TRY IT ON!

DISTINGUISHING BETWEEN ISTP AND ISTJ

Which temperament seems like the best fit and why? Improviser (ISTP) or Stabilizer (ISTJ)?

_____

_____

Which information gathering function-attitude appears the best fit and why? Experiencing (Se) or Recalling (Si)?

_____

_____

Which decision making function-attitude appears the best fit and why? Analyzing (Ti) or Systematizing (Te)?

_____

_____

What developmental factors might be relevant in selecting best-fit type?

_____

_____

3. DISTINGUISHING INFJ FROM INTJ

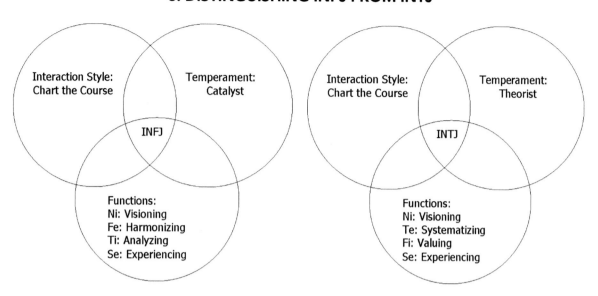

INFJs and INTJs share certain **core similarities**. With an **Introverting** preference, using their first function-attitude in the internal world, their energy tends to move in first to reflect before moving out to the external world for interaction. Both types have the same Adult function, **Visioning (Ni)** which means they gravitate towards conceptual data which they correlate unconsciously over a period of time, and which then comes into consciousness as an "aha" or sudden insight. They both share an **iNtuiting** preference which means that they tend to naturally gravitate towards concepts, models and ideas, before focusing on specifics. They both share the **Judging** preference so they tend to look for closure and stick with decisions once they are made. Finally, both types use the **Chart the Course** Interaction Style: which means that they share the same theme of wanting a course of action to follow. They tend to allow others to make the first move in initiating relationships. They both tend to identify a process to accomplish a goal and like to make informed deliberate decisions. They share a drive to anticipate and plan ahead to get the desired result, and can be stressed when they cannot foresee future direction.

However, there are also a number of **marked differences** between **INFJs** and **INTJs**:

INFJ	INTJ
Temperament	
INFJs have a **Catalyst** temperament. Catalysts need a sense of purpose and meaning, and tend to be on a constant quest for unique identity. They value authentic relationships and collaboration, and employ empathy in their interaction with others. They view the world as a journey towards self-actualization, with a constant eye to people and emotions.	**INTJs** have a **Theorist** temperament. Theorists need to be an expert and demonstrate competence, and tend to be on a constant search for knowledge in whatever ventures they deem important. They value autonomy and independence in their activities, and employ intellectual rigour in their approach to facts and data. They view the world from a strategic perspective, with a constant eye on logical ramifications and the relationships between means and end.
Stress Response Each stress response can cause the temperament to act diametrically differently from their innate abilities.	
Catalysts (INFJ) may emotionally disconnect, use selective interpretation, and over-generalise a negative situation. The paradox of this stress response is that they move from empathetic to unfeeling.	**Theorists (INTJ)** may over use critical questioning if they perceive themselves to have failed and "nit-pick" details. The paradox of this stress response is to move from rational to irrational.

INFJ	INTJ
Decision Making Functions	
INFJs use **Harmonizing (Fe)**. They like to make decisions to achieve consensus and are gifted at creating a safe environment. Using Harmonizing, they are adept at self-disclosing to connect with others, may show their emotions on their face (on good and bad days!), and may struggle when there is an extreme conflict.	**INTJs** use **Systematizing (Te)**. They like to make objective decisions using causal-effect logic and are adept at organizing information and resources in the most efficient way to achieve the end goal. Using Systematizing they can establish clear boundaries of "right" and "wrong", are adept at creating flow charts, and may sometimes appear a little too direct.

General Observations	
Catalysts (INFJ) tend to use **Integrative Thinking**: where similarities behind different data or points of view are naturally connected. As a result, their language may include non-sequiturs, as they link data that is not immediately obvious.	**Theorists (INTJ)** tend to use **Differential Thinking**: where distinctions in points of view are seen first. As a result, their language may include analytical questions to more thoroughly define and explore these dissimilarities.
Catalysts (INFJ) tend to use **global language** including such words as never, always, etc. while demonstrating interpersonal awareness. Their words will include mention of impressions, with no specific examples.	**Theorists (INTJ)** tend to use **precise language**: with exactly the right word for the specific situation. Words are their tools, so they will often correct word choice to ascertain that their understanding is accurate.

INFJ	INTJ
General Observations Continued	
INFJs tend to value **empathic** relationships and work best in an environment that has **cooperative interaction**. In addition **INFJs** naturally consider the people and subjective elements (**Feeling** preference) and see the exceptions to the rule. **INFJs** tend to give **positive feedback** as they focus on developing an individual's potential, however, for the same reason, they may struggle with providing accurate developmental feedback.	**INTJs** tend to value **expert** relationships and work best in an environment that has **intellectual rigour** and challenge In addition **INTJs** naturally consider the reason and objective elements (**Thinking** preference) and search for logical consistency. **INTJs** tend to provide **developmental feedback** as they focus on improving performance and may view positive feedback as redundant; "Of course you are doing well – I would tell you if you weren't!"

QUESTIONS FOR SORTING BETWEEN CATALYST AND THEORIST TEMPERAMENTS

What drives you? What do you really enjoy doing?

- Listen for the **Catalyst's (INFJ)** drive for meaning and significance, and to be seen as special.
- Listen for the **Theorist's (INTJ)** drive for competence, autonomy, and being an expert.

What do you really struggle with? When was a time that you felt you had failed?

- Listen for **Catalysts (INFJ)** to describe failure as being betrayed, being made to feel undervalued, receiving no positive feedback, or lots of developmental feedback.
- Listen for **Theorists (INTJ)** to describe situations when they thought they had failed on two or more fronts, where they had no autonomy or ability to influence future outcomes.

QUESTIONS FOR CLARIFYING TEMPERAMENT VIA PRAGMATISM OR COLLABORATION

How important is it to do what is necessary to achieve the goal, even if people are not necessarily on the same page?

- If it is important, consider **INTJ**, because **Theorists** tend to be more pragmatic at doing what it takes to achieve the goal.
- If people are important, consider **INFJ** because **Catalysts** will naturally want to build an element of consensus into achieving the goal.

QUESTIONS FOR SORTING BETWEEN HARMONIZING (FE) AND SYSTEMATIZING (TE) FUNCTION-ATTITUDES

When you are faced with a conflict, how comfortable are you in addressing that conflict?

- If Comfortable, consider **INTJ**, because **Theorists** using **Systematizing (Te)** tend to be comfortable "calling a spade a spade" and would rather address the conflict in order to improve the overall performance of the system. As they mature, they may access their Child **Valuing (Fi)** function-attitude and appear more tuned in to fairness alongside logic.
- If Not Comfortable, consider **INFJ** because **Catalysts** using **Harmonizing (Fe)** tend to find conflict stressful and may avoid addressing the issue hoping that it will resolve itself in order to improve the overall group dynamic. As they mature, they may access their Child **Analyzing (Ti)** function-attitude and appear more logical in reframing and addressing conflict situations.

Are you clear on boundaries in the external world – who does what, what you do and what you don't do?

- If you are clear, consider **INTJ**, because **Theorists** using **Systematizing (Te)** tend to be able to set clear boundaries with others with little feeling of discomfort. The clear definition of roles smoothes the operation of the system.

- If you struggle with setting clear boundaries, consider **INFJ** because **Catalysts** using **Harmonizing (Fe)** tend to prefer to build consensus and may feel discomfort trying to map out detailed steps and accountabilities.

3. Distinguishing INFJ from INTJ: Review

EXERCISE 10: DISTINGUISHING BETWEEN INFJ AND INTJ

Thinking of these two personality types:
- Which temperament seems like the best fit and why? Catalyst (INFJ) or Theorist (INTJ)?
- Which decision making function-attitude appears the best fit? Harmonizing (Fe) or Systematizing (Te)?
- What developmental factors might be relevant in selecting best-fit type?

TRY IT ON!

DISTINGUISHING BETWEEN INFJ AND INTJ

Which temperament seems like the best fit and why? Catalyst (INFJ) or Theorist (INTJ)?

_____

_____

Which decision making function-attitude appears the best fit? Harmonizing (Fe) or Systematizing (Te)?

_____

_____

What developmental factors might be relevant in selecting best-fit type?

_____

_____

4. DISTINGUISHING ISFJ FROM INFJ

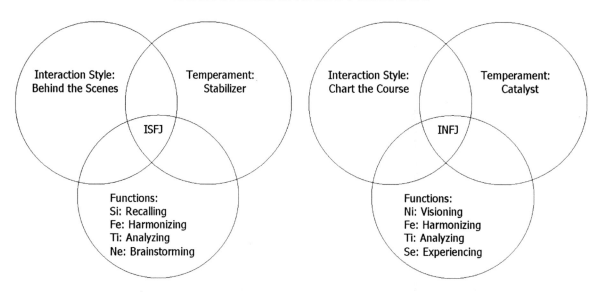

ISFJs and INFJs share certain **core similarities.** Both types tend to prefer to use **Harmonizing (Fe)** to make decisions in the external world and therefore can appear gentle and empathetic. Both share a natural interest and concern in ensuring the group process is productive. Using Harmonizing as a Parent function, they will have an innate ability to create a safe environment and individuals will tend to feel validated. In addition, they both share the **Judging** preference, which means that they like to push for closure in the external world rather than going with the flow. They both view time as a finite resource and like to make a plan and adhere to it. Both types value interpersonal relationships: ISFJs want to be part of a team, INFJs like meaningful one-on-one interactions. Finally, both types share the **Introverting** preference, which means that they tend to wait for others to take the first move in initiating relationships. They naturally go inwards first to gather information before circling out to make decisions externally. They may both tend to use more reserved body language and listen more than talk.

Despite these similarities, however, there are also a number of **marked differences** between **ISFJs** and **INFJs:**

ISFJ	INFJ
Temperament	
ISFJs have a **Stabilizer** temperament. Stabilizers need to know what they are responsible for, and like to live up to these responsibilities. Stabilizers tend to be collaborative with other team mates, and enjoy instituting processes to achieve structure and stability. Stabilizers tend to enjoy being part of a team and contributing to accomplishment of concrete goals.	**INFJs** have a **Catalyst** temperament. Catalysts need a sense of purpose and meaning, and tend to be on a constant quest for unique identity. Catalysts tend to value authentic relationships and collaboration, and employ empathy in their interaction with others. Catalysts tend to view the world as a journey towards self-actualisation, with a constant eye to people and emotions.
ISFJ	INFJ
Stress Response Each stress response can cause the temperament to act diametrically differently from their innate abilities.	
Stabilizers (ISFJ) may tend to play a "doormat" game when they find themselves overloaded; letting go of tasks and allowing others to make all the decisions. The paradox of this stress response is that they move from responsible to irresponsible.	Catalysts (INFJ) may tend to live in their own world and withdraw when they feel like they have been betrayed. The paradox of this stress response is that they move from having authentic relationships to conducting inauthentic interactions.

ISFJ	INFJ
Interaction Style	
ISFJ's Interaction Style is **Behind-the-Scenes™**. This means that they naturally want to integrate as much information as possible and use a consultative decision making style to achieve the best result. With a Behind-the-Scenes™ style, ISFJs tend to support and protect by going the extra mile to ensure people are accommodated. The Behind-the-Scenes™ energy appears patient, approachable and gentle.	INFJ's Interaction Style is **Chart-the-Course™**. This means that they naturally want to anticipate future direction and plan a course of action and use deliberate decision making to achieve a desired result. With a Chart the Course style INFJs tend to develop people to achieve their purpose and implement programs to make a difference The Chart-the-Course™ energy appears focused, intense and reserved.

Preference for Directing or Informing	
The Behind the Scenes Style™ tends to prefer getting buy-in to the goal or process and uses an **Informing** style of communication. This may involve making statements, asking for input and suggesting ideas in a non-directive way.	The Chart the Course style tends to prefer completing the task in a timely manner and uses a **Directing** style of communication. This may involve giving advice, being explicit about outcomes and telling others about ideas and actions.

ISFJ	INFJ
General Observations (Communication Style)	
The **sequential communication** style that Stabilizers (ISFJ) use will often include a beginning, middle and end, with a step-by-step pacing. Common words and expressions could include "in my experience", "in the past", "better than", "worse than."	The **global communication** style that Catalysts (INFJ) use will often include metaphors, generalizations and impressions. Common words and expressions could include "everyone", "always'" "never", "I just have this feeling."
Information Gathering Function-Attitudes	
ISFJs use **Recalling (Si)** to gather data. When required to begin a new activity, they tend to go back in time to think of what worked and what didn't work, and look at what they would do differently this time. Using Recalling in this way often means that they have a clear sense of what is real or practical in any situation—although that can also manifest itself in appearing negative: "that did not work before."	**INFJs** use **Visioning (Ni)** to gather data. When required to begin a new activity, they tend to gravitate towards conceptual data which they correlate unconsciously over a period of time, and which then comes into consciousness as an 'aha' or sudden insight. Using Visioning in this way will often mean that they are astute in seeing breakthrough solutions and ideas that appear unrelated to the original data- although this can sound unrealistic as there is no obvious link between the data gathered and the solution.

QUESTIONS FOR SORTING BETWEEN STABILIZER AND CATALYST TEMPERAMENTS

What drives you? What do you really enjoy doing?

- Listen for the **Stabilizer's (ISFJ)** drive for responsibility, membership, belonging to the team, and concrete goal achievement.
- Listen for the **Catalyst's (INFJ)** drive for meaning and significance, and to be seen as special.

What do you really struggle with? When was a time that you felt you had failed?

- Listen for **Stabilizers (ISFJ)** to describe projects where no one lived up to their responsibilities, where there was constant change and no sense of teamwork.
- Listen for **Catalysts (INFJ)** to describe failure as being betrayed, being made to feel undervalued, receiving no positive feedback, or lots of developmental feedback.

Do you tend to be risk-averse? Do you tend to put in contingency plans to protect against things going wrong?

- If **Yes,** consider **ISFJ** because **Stabilizers** tend to be more cautious, and are adept at planning for things that might go wrong.
- If **No,** consider **INFJ** because **Catalysts**, with their innate sense of hope, tend to be more credulous, believing things will go right despite outstanding evidence to the contrary.

QUESTIONS FOR CLARIFYING INFORMATION-GATHERING FUNCTION-ATTITUDES

To what extent do you refer back to past data when beginning a new project?

- If **Yes,** consider **ISFJ** because **Stabilizers** using **Recalling (Si)** tend to be past-focused, using what happened in the past to compare and contrast current reality with past experience.
- If **No,** consider **INFJ** because **Catalysts** using **Visioning (Ni)** tend to be future-focused, envisioning a future goal and then mapping out the flow to achieve this outcome.

To what extent are you uncomfortable with change?

- If **Yes,** consider **ISFJ** because **Stabilizers** tend to be more uncomfortable with change, as they value preservation of social groups and security.
- If **No,** consider **INFJ** because **Catalysts** tend to more comfortable with change, as they value self actualisation and meaningful relationships; both of which may involve making changes.

QUESTIONS FOR CLARIFYING INTERACTION STYLE

Are you stressed by not being given enough time or credit?

- If **Yes,** consider **ISFJ** because **Behind-the-Scenes™ Stabilizers** tend to be stressed when pressured to decide too quickly, and when they are not given enough time or credit.
- If **No** consider **INFJ** because **Chart-the-Course™ Catalysts** tend to be stressed by not knowing what will happen and when they do not clearly see the steps towards the goal.

Is progress towards the goal really important to you?

- If **Yes**, consider **INFJ** because **Chart-the-Course™ Catalyst's** focus is on having controlled movement towards the goal.
- If **No**, consider **ISFJ** because **Behind-the-Scenes™ Stabilizers** tend to delay taking action until they are sure there will be a quality outcome, and therefore will not follow the process until they are sure it will create the best result.

4. Distinguishing ISFJ from INFJ: Review

EXERCISE 11: DISTINGUISHING BETWEEN ISFJ AND INFJ

Thinking of these two personality types:

- Which temperament seems like the best fit and why? Stabilizer (ISFJ) or Catalyst (INFJ)?
- Which information gathering function-attitude appears the best fit and why? Recalling (Si) or Visioning (Ni)?
- Which Interaction Style appears the best fit and why? Behind the Scenes or Chart the Course?
- What developmental factors might be relevant in selecting best-fit type?

TRY IT ON!

DISTINGUISHING BETWEEN ISFJ AND INFJ

Which temperament seems like the best fit and why? Stabilizer (ISFJ) or Catalyst (INFJ)?

_____

_____

Which information gathering function-attitude appears the best fit and why? Recalling (Si) or Visioning (Ni)?

_____

_____

Which Interaction Style appears the best fit and why? Behind the Scenes or Chart the Course?

_____

_____

What developmental factors might be relevant in selecting best-fit type?

_____

_____

5. DISTINGUISHING ISFJ FROM ISFP

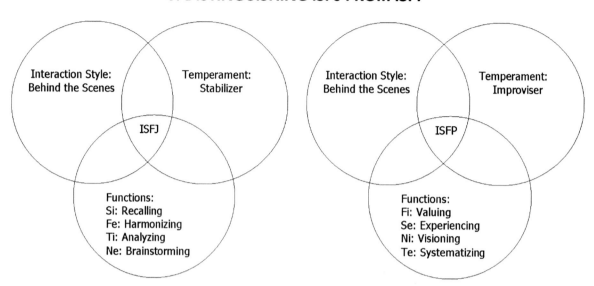

ISFJs and ISFPs share certain **core similarities** because they both tend to be gentle, interested in people and grounded in concrete reality. Both types like to achieve tangible goals and consider people in making decisions. Both share the **Introverting** preference which means that they reflect first and they use their First/Adult function internally. Both share the **Sensing** preference and therefore tend to naturally communicate using concrete language which may include stories, examples and specifics. Both types use the **Feeling** preference to make decisions and will therefore tend to focus on human needs, values and harmony. Also both types share the **Behind the Scenes** Interaction Style when communicating and influencing others. This Style is characterized by allowing digressions in discussions and supporting a facilitative process in order to get the best result possible. They will take the time necessary to consult with others and integrate relevant data, although the final decision tends to be made by them and not with the group. Their energy tends to appear as patient and unassuming, which may attract others to share their ideas and thoughts with them. They prefer to share information by making statements or observations (**Informing**) versus providing instructions (**Directing**). They both tend to let others take the first move, responding to others openings, rather than initiating interaction themselves.

Despite these similarities, however, there are also a number of **marked differences** between **ISFJs** and **ISFPs**. Next a few of these indicators are highlighted:

ISFJ	ISFP
Temperament	
ISFJs have a **Stabilizer** temperament. Stabilizers need to know what they are responsible for, and like to live up to these responsibilities. Stabilizers tend to want to be part of a team, and enjoy contributing to concrete goal accomplishment. Stabilizers tend to be collaborative with other teammates, and enjoy instituting processes to build structure and stability.	ISFPs have an **Improviser** temperament. Improvisers need freedom, the ability to act in the moment and enjoy the here and now. Improvisers tend to make the most of any situation and are talented at seizing current opportunities. Improvisers tend to read team mates well because they innately recognise the motive of the other person and can usually figure out how to get their needs and the other person's needs met.
Stress Response Each stress response can cause the temperament to act diametrically differently from their innate abilities.	
Stabilizers (ISFJ) may tend to play a "doormat" game when they find themselves overloaded, letting go of tasks and allowing others to make all the decisions. The paradox of this stress response is that they move from responsible to irresponsible.	**Improvisers (ISFP)** may deliberately miss deadlines or use deceptive agendas to cause a reaction when they are feeling confined or bored. The paradox of this stress response is to move from graceful to disgraceful.

ISFJ	ISFP
Information Gathering Function-Attitudes	
ISFJs use **Recalling (Si)** to **perceive information.** When required to begin a new activity, they tend to go back in time, to think of what worked and what didn't work, and look at what they would do differently this time. Using **Recalling (Si)** in this way may often mean that they have a clear sense of what is real or practical in any given situation. They also tend to compare and contrast current with past data and use "ranking" words: higher than, bigger than, better than, etc.	**ISFPs** use **Experiencing (Se)** to **perceive information.** When required to begin a new activity, they tend to read all the concrete data in the moment – sound, sight, smell, taste, and touch and look at feasible options. Using **Experiencing (Se)** in this way may often mean that they have a clear sense of what the best thing to do right now would be in any given situation. They also tend to use more informal language, often including action words and those that paint a vivid mental picture.

ISFJ	ISFP
Decision Making Function-Attitudes	
ISFJs use **Harmonizing (Fe)** to make decisions. Harmonizing (Fe) involves making subjective decisions to optimize interpersonal harmony and those using this function-attitude are often gifted at creating a safe environment where others feel comfortable in expressing opinions. Using Harmonizing (Fe) with ease, individuals may tend to demonstrate warm and welcoming body language as they are driven to achieve consensus.	**ISFPs** use **Valuing (Fi)** to make decisions. Valuing (Fi) involves making subjective decisions to value diversity using an internal belief system and those using this function-attitude often are tolerant and supportive of individual differences. Using Valuing (Fi) with ease individuals tend to be private in sharing their innermost thoughts, and driven to live their life in alignment with their own internal values.

ISFJ	ISFP
Adult Function	
ISFJ's Adult function is **Recalling (Si)**. This means that naturally ISFJ's energy will direct inwards first to their rich historic databank of sensory information, Recalling (Si), and then move outwards to make decisions to optimize the group dynamic, Harmonizing (Fe). As a result they may appear more structured and planful.	**ISFP's Adult** function is **Valuing (Fi)**. This means that naturally ISFP's energy will direct inwards to consider what is fair in a given situation by accessing their Valuing (Fi) function, and then move outwards to gather and manage sensory data in the now moment, Experiencing (Se). As a result they may appear more open and flexible.
General Observations	
ISFJs tend to support team members in achieving the goal. Their **sequential communication** style will often include a beginning, middle and end, with a step-by-step pacing. Common words and expressions include "in my experience", 'in the past'" etc.	**ISFPs** tend to provide support to individuals that they value. Their **concise colourful language** will often get to the point quickly and be more literal and specific. Their unembellished communication style tends to "cut through" unnecessary detail.

QUESTIONS FOR SORTING BETWEEN STABILIZER AND IMPROVISER TEMPERAMENTS

What drives you? What do you really enjoy doing?

- Listen for the **Stabilizer's (ISFJ)** drive for responsibility, membership, belonging to the team, and concrete goal achievement.
- Listen for the **Improviser's (ISFP)** drive for freedom, fun and seeing results in the moment, making an impact and being noticed.

What do you really struggle with? When was a time that you felt you had failed?

- Listen for **Stabilizers (ISFJ)** to describe projects where no one lived up to their responsibilities, where there was constant change, and no sense of teamwork.
- Listen for **Improvisers (ISFP)** to describe long-term projects, with no tangible outcome, too many rules, and pointless details.

Do you like to see immediate concrete results from your efforts?

- If **No**, consider **ISFJ**, because **Stabilizers** tend to enjoy achieving the "right" concrete results and will plan and sequence activities accordingly. They want to do it right first time.
- If **Yes** consider **ISFP**, because **Improvisers** tend to press for immediate action: let's do it, and often prefer to react afterwards to correct any mistakes if necessary.

QUESTIONS FOR CLARIFYING RECALLING (SI) OR EXPERIENCING (SE)

When you are starting a new project, do you tend to go back to what you did last time, so that you can compare and contrast what worked then?

- If **Yes** consider **Stabilizer (ISFJ)**, because Stabilizers, using **Recalling (Si)**, will normally track back in time to think about what was done in what sequence, and then think about how it could be applied in the current context.
- If **No**, consider **Improviser (ISFP)**, because Improvisers **using Experiencing (Se)** tend to jump in and focus more on the here and now, without necessarily considering past data, as they trust their talent of being able to respond in the moment.

If necessary, are you willing to engage in tough discussions in order to achieve the "right" decisions?

- If **No**, consider **Stabilizer (ISFJ)**, because Stabilizers, using **Harmonizing (Fe)**, will normally try to avoid conflict and work to gain agreement. Achieving the best overall decision will often take precedence over individual beliefs.
- If **Yes**, consider **Improviser (ISFP)**, because Improvisers using **Valuing (Fi)** can be easy going and people focused, but will often stand up strongly if a decision is not in alignment with internal values.

5. Distinguishing ISFJ from ISFP: Review

EXERCISE 12: DISTINGUISHING BETWEEN ISFJ AND ISFP

Thinking of these two personality types:

- Which temperament seems like the best fit and why? Stabilizer (ISFJ) or Improviser (ISFP)?
- Which information gathering function-attitude appears the best fit and why? Recalling (Si) or Experiencing (Se)?
- Which decision making function-attitude appears the best fit and why? Harmonizing (Fe) or Valuing (Fi)?
- What developmental factors might be relevant in selecting best-fit type?

TRY IT ON!

DISTINGUISHING BETWEEN ISFJ AND ISFP

Which temperament seems like the best fit and why? Stabilizer (ISFJ) or Improviser (ISFP)?

_____

_____

Which information gathering function-attitude appears the best fit and why? Recalling (Si) or Experiencing (Se)?

_____

_____

Which decision making function-attitude appears the best fit and why? Harmonizing (Fe) or Valuing (Fi)?

_____

_____

What developmental factors might be relevant in selecting best-fit type?

_____

_____

6. DISTINGUISHING ISTP FROM INTP

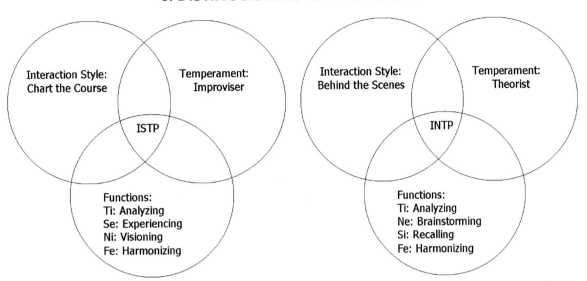

INTPs and ISTPs share certain **core similarities** because they both tend to be intensely analytical and logical. They make decisions using the same adult function: **Analyzing (Ti).** This means that they are driven to dissect and categorize data, evaluating it against internal criteria, and make independent decisions using this mental model. Those who use Analyzing (Ti) with ease excel at examining an argument, creating a unique point of view, and reframing problems from various logical perspectives. They will often use critical questioning to check the accuracy of a point of view. In addition they will tend to approach people and events as objective observers as they internally evaluate pros and cons. Both types share an **Introverting** preference and will tend to reflect before taking action. They may tend to pause before they respond as they sort and refine their analytical frameworks. They both tend to wait for the other person to initiate an interaction when communicating with others. Both types share the **Perceiving** preference and tend to view time as an infinite resource; either changing decisions as new data becomes available or in being comfortable with a lack of closure.

However, despite these similarities there are also a number of **marked differences** between ISTPs and INTPs. The following highlights a few of these key indicators.

ISTP	INTP
Temperament	
ISTPs have an **Improviser** temperament. Improvers are driven by the need for freedom and to take action. They tend to like to enjoy the here and now and are driven to be impressive. Improvisers tend to make the most of any situation and are talented at seizing current opportunities. Improvisers use this **tactical skill set** to read the current context and skilfully manage the situation.	**INTPs** have a **Theorist** temperament. Theorists are driven by the need to be knowledgeable and competent and retain their intellectual independence. They tend to have an infinite time orientation and are driven to see things from a strategic, long-term perspective. Theorists tend to use logic and expertise and are talented at abstractly assessing a situation and thinking through unexpected possibilities. Theorists use this **strategic skill set** to integrate ideas into cohesive innovative theories.
Stress Response Each stress response can cause the temperament to act diametrically differently from their innate abilities.	
Improvisers (ISTP) may leave projects to the last minute to appear impressive, causing an impact to others. The paradox of this stress response is to move from graceful to disgraceful.	**Theorists (INTP)** may become absorbed in their analysis and make decisions overly complex resulting in no action. The paradox of this stress response is to move from rational to irrational.

ISTP	INTP
Information Gathering Function-Attitudes	
ISTPs use **Experiencing (Se)**. They tend to read all the concrete data in the moment – sound, sight, smell, taste, and touch. Using Experiencing (Se) in this way will often mean they will pick up options for current action and tactical solutions to problems. They are gifted at making ideas concrete and real. They may however miss reading between the lines and instead take a situation at face value.	**INTPs** use **Brainstorming (Ne)**. They tend to read between the lines and infer meaning from data. Using Brainstorming (Ne) in this way will often mean that they are able to see patterns and possibilities that are not immediately obvious when solving problems. They are gifted at creating new ideas without limit. They may however miss considering the concrete reality and dismiss concerns about practicality.

General Observations	
ISTPs tend to show an interest in practical reality and having fun with people, tools and models, versus hypothesizing about concepts. Their **concise, colourful** language will tend to get to the point quickly, and will often be used to amuse colleagues and friends. Their literal communication style tends to "cut through" unnecessary detail.	INTPs tend to enjoy the pursuit of intellectual purity through extensive exploration of concepts and hypotheses, versus discussions about tangible specifics. Their **precise, accurate** language will tend to clarify and define data clearly and may result in correcting the word choice of others for greater clearness. Their critical questioning can help to anticipate and overcome potential challenges.

ISTP	INTP
Interaction Style	
ISTPs use the **Chart the Course Interaction Style.** This means that they are driven to anticipate future situations and wish to drive actions in a thought-through way towards a desired result ISTP's Chart the Course style specializes in setting quick reference points and then using the tools available to get results. Chart the Course energy appears more focused, intense and calm.	INTPs use the **Behind the Scenes Interaction Style.** This means that that they are driven to consult as many points of view as possible to integrate data in order to get the best result possible. INTP's Behind the Scenes style specializes in clearly defining specifications and bringing clarity to a situation by solidifying a new approach. Behind the Scenes energy appears more patient, unassuming and approachable.
Preference for Directing or Informing	
ISTPs tend to want to innately use a more **Directing** communication style to achieve the task. ISTPs will probably feel more comfortable giving clear statements and instructions to ensure clarity of action.	INTPs tend to want to innately use a more **Informing** communication style to solicit input and buy-in from others. INTPs will probably feel more comfortable soliciting input, asking for ideas and making suggestions to ensure group buy-in.

QUESTIONS FOR SORTING BETWEEN IMPROVISER AND THEORIST TEMPERAMENTS

What drives you? What do you really enjoy doing? What was your best job?

- Listen for **Improviser's (ISTP)** drive for freedom, fun and seeing results in the moment, making an impact and being noticed.
- Listen for the **Theorist's (INTP)** drive for competence, intellectual rigor, knowledge acquisition and strategic focus.

What do you really struggle with? When was a time that you felt you had failed?

- Listen for **Improvisers (ISTP)** to describe long-term projects, with no tangible outcome, too many rules, and pointless details.
- Listen for **Theorists (INTP)** to describe failure as perceiving themselves to have said or done something that was stupid or to have obviously failed. INTPs may also struggle with the implementation of ideas (an area where ISTPs excel).

QUESTIONS TO CLARIFY TEMPERAMENT VIA CURRENT OR FUTURE DIRECTION

Do you need to see immediate concrete results from your efforts?

- If **Yes**, consider **ISTP** because **Improvisers** tend to drive toward tangible results. As they mature, ISTPs may also talk about getting an "aha" (Child **Visioning Ni** function) and then making it happen (supporting **Experiencing Se** as the Adult.)
- If **No**, consider **INTP** because **Theorists** tend to enjoy exploring ideas and concepts without the need to see tangible outcomes immediately. As they mature INTPs may talk more about what is real and concrete as they access their Child function **Recalling (Si)**.

Do you tend to focus on the here and now? Do you trust the future to take care of itself?

- If **Yes** consider **Improviser (ISTP)** because Improvisers tend to live in the present, seize the moment and trust the future to look after itself.
- If **No** consider **Theorist (INTP)** because Theorists tend to have an infinite time orientation: anything is possible in the future – often neglecting practical evidence to the contrary!

| QUESTIONS TO IDENTIFY EXPERIENCING (SE) VERSUS BRAINSTORMING (NE) |

Are you tuned in to physical changes of body language? Are you easily distracted by your environment?

- If **Yes** consider **Improviser (ISTP)** because Improvisers using **Experiencing (Se)** tend to pick up changes in the external environment and enjoy making things real.
- If **No** consider **Theorist (INTP)** because Theorists using **Brainstorming (Ne)** may tend to be more oblivious to physical clues as they focus on strategy and future direction.

| QUESTIONS TO CLARIFY INTERACTION STYLE |

Are you comfortable in "Tell" mode?

- If **Yes,** consider **Improviser (ISTP)** because Improvisers using **Directing** communication prefer to be explicit about who they want to do what by when.
- If **No,** consider **Theorist (INTP)** because Theorists using **Informing** communication prefer to give information to motivate to action, rather than telling.

Is quality of the end result more important than progress towards the goal for you?

- If **Yes,** consider **INTP** because the **Behind-the-Scenes**™ **Theorist** will not want to take action because the focus is on incorporating ideas into a new unified rationale or model.
- If **No** consider **ISTP** because the **Chart-the-Course**™ **Improviser** will want to take action because the focus is on progress towards the goal.

6. Distinguishing ISTP from INTP: Review

EXERCISE 13: DISTINGUISHING BETWEEN ISTP AND INTP

Thinking of these two personality types:

- Which temperament seems like the best fit and why? Improviser (ISTP) or Theorist (INTP)?
- Which information gathering function-attitude appears the best fit and why? Experiencing (Se) or Brainstorming (Ne)?
- Which Interaction Style appears the best fit and why? Chart the Course or Behind the Scenes?
- What developmental factors might be relevant in selecting best-fit type?

TRY IT ON!

DISTINGUISHING BETWEEN ISTP AND INTP

Which temperament seems like the best fit and why? Improviser (ISTP) or Theorist (INTP)?

_____

_____

Which information gathering function-attitude appears the best fit and why? Experiencing (Se) or Brainstorming (Ne)?

_____

_____

Which Interaction Style appears the best fit and why? Chart the Course or Behind the Scenes?

_____

_____

What developmental factors might be relevant in selecting best-fit type?

_____

_____

7. DISTINGUISHING INTP FROM INFP

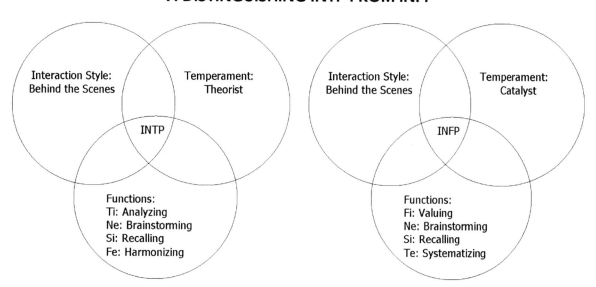

There are several **key similarities** between **INTP**s and **INFP**s. Both share the **Behind the Scenes"** Interaction Style. Individuals who use this style when trying to influence others tend to wait for others to take the first step when interacting, and prefer to share information with others in an informing, non-directive way. As a result, they both tend to appear unassuming, accommodating, and approachable. They like to take time to integrate all data before making a decision in order to achieve the best possible result. The both tend to make consultative decisions, gathering input from multiple sources before taking a step back and making the final decision themselves. In addition, both types share the **Introverting** preference, which means that, energy flows to the internal world first. Both tend to reflect before acting, and there may be less obvious restrained body language. Both types **use Brainstorming (Ne)** as their Parent function which means they are adept at inferring possibilities, seeing patterns and meaning and reading between the lines. Both types tend to prefer abstract data, (**iNtuiting** preference) and move from big picture to specifics. In addition, as both share the **Perceiving** preference, they tend to be flexible, open-ended and comfortable with adapting to new situations.

However, despite these **similarities** there are also a number of **marked differences** between **INTPs** and **INFPs.** The following table highlights a few of these key indicators.

INTP	INFP
Temperament	
INTPs have a **Theorist** temperament. Theorists are driven by a need to be knowledgeable and competent and want to retain their intellectual independence. They tend see things from a strategic, logical, long-term perspective and value **expert relationships**. Theorists tend to appear as more aloof to others based on their needs for autonomy and control.	**INFPs** have a **Catalyst** temperament. Catalysts are driven by a need to be unique or special and want a sense of purpose and meaning. They tend to see bridges between apparently disparate points of view and value **empathic relationships**. Catalysts tend to work well with individuals as they use empathy to put themselves into other people's shoes.
Stress Response Each stress response can cause the temperament to act diametrically differently from their innate abilities.	
Theorists (INTP) may become "preoccupied" and appear emotionally distant. They may pull back internally to focus on their perceived failure and overly complicate issues. The paradox of this stress response is that they move from rational to irrational.	Catalysts (INFP) may project negative attributions to others and read pessimistically between the lines. The paradox of this stress response is to move from authentic to inauthentic relationships.

INTP	INFP
Decision Making Function-Attitudes	
INTPs use **Analyzing (Ti)** as an Adult function which involves making decisions by evaluating data and defining situations against internal logical criteria. Those who use Analyzing (Ti) with ease excel at density of definition both of words and the current situation. They use critical questioning to dissect and argue a point of view, thereby bringing the gift of intellectual clarity, new arguments or solutions. Sometimes though this ability to stay with a topic until comprehended may alienate other types as it appears to be excessive analyzing.	**INFPs** use **Valuing (Fi)** as an Adult function which involves making decisions by evaluating data and defining situations against an internal beliefs system. Those who use Valuing (Fi) with ease hold on to their integrity and truth in a constant quest for ensuring their decisions in the external world mesh with their internal values. They are conscientious at exploring situations from multiple perspectives and tend to be private in sharing their innermost thoughts. Sometimes though this reflection can cause them to delay or struggle with major decisions.

INTP	INFP
Hierarchy of Function-Attitudes	
INTPs use **Harmonizing (Fe)** as a Fourth function balancing their Adult Analyzing (Ti). They will therefore tend to be aware of subjective criteria to optimize group interaction and appear laid back and empathetic. Using Harmonizing (Fe) in this way, they are able to understand the greater personal issues that might be outside of the Analyzing (Ti) logic. Under stress however they may be oblivious to what is appropriate for group interaction.	**INFPs** use **Systematizing (Te)** as a Fourth function balancing their Adult Valuing (Fi). They will therefore tend to make some decisions using logical criteria to plan and organize logistics and events in the external world. Using Systematizing (Te) in this way, they are able to give directives for actions which are in support of their cause. Under stress however, when their values are crossed, they may obsess about details and achieving structure, and be overly direct in standing up for their principles.
General Observations	
INTPs enjoy the pursuit of intellectual purity through extensive exploration of concepts and hypotheses. Their **precise language** will often show when they correct the word choice of others and expose new ideas to extensive critical questioning. In debate, they may have difficulty accepting data that is contrary to their mental model.	**INFPs** enjoy learning about the theory of human behaviours, particularly in helping people get more out of life. Their **global language** will often include generalizations and talk about impressions versus specifics. Their more flowing style may appear to "meander" and include non-sequitors. This more abstract communication style can appear "fluffy" or unrealistic.

QUESTIONS FOR SORTING BETWEEN THEORIST AND CATALYST TEMPERAMENTS

What drives you? What do you really enjoy doing?

- Listen **for Catalyst's (INFP)** need for significant relationships and drive to develop people and their potential.
- Listen for the **Theorist's (INTP)** need for competence, intellectual independence, and strategic focus.

What do you really struggle with? When was a time that you felt you had failed?

- Listen for **Theorists (INTP)** to describe failure as perceiving themselves to have said or done something that was stupid or to have been unsuccessful in two or more areas. INTPs may also struggle with feeling out of control and having no challenge or independence.

- Listen for **Catalysts (INFP)** to describe failure as being betrayed, being made to act against their beliefs or receiving no positive feedback. INFPs may also struggle with feeling undervalued and receiving only developmental feedback.

Do you always tend to see the impact on people when making decisions?
- If **Yes,** consider **INFP** because **Catalysts** tend to consider the emotional issues, and want decisions to be fair to those involved.
- If **No,** consider **INTP** because **Theorists** tend to focus on the logical principles first and approach decisions more pragmatically.

Are you aware of how people are responding to you?
- If **Yes,** consider **Catalyst (INFP)** because Catalysts using empathy tend to be very aware of individual responses to any given situation.
- If **No,** consider **Theorist (INTP)** because Theorists may tend to be oblivious of interpersonal dynamics as they focus on the logical outcomes to any given situation.

Do you tend to see life as a journey towards a goal?
- If **Yes,** consider **Catalyst (INFP)** because Catalysts tend to be future focused and are on a constant journey to achieve their purpose.
- If **No,** consider **Theorist (INTP)** because Theorists tend to have an infinite time orientation so are constantly scanning past, present and future for the most relevant data to improve a system or theory.

Do you tend to be naturally sceptical and accept very little on faith?
- If **Yes,** consider **Theorist (INTP)** because Theorists tend to take a theoretical and logical stance and require objective proof for new concepts and models.
- If **No,** consider **Catalyst (INFP)** because Catalysts tend to take a credulous stance and begin with a position of faith first before requiring evidence.

7. Distinguishing INTP from INFP: Review

EXERCISE 14: DISTINGUISHING BETWEEN INTP AND INFP

Thinking of these two personality types:

- Which temperament seems like the best fit and why? Theorist (INTP) or Catalyst (INFP)?
- Which decision making function-attitude appears the best fit and why? Analyzing (Ti) or Valuing (Fi)?
- What developmental factors might be relevant in selecting best-fit type?

TRY IT ON!

DISTINGUISHING BETWEEN INTP AND INFP

Which temperament seems like the best fit and why? Theorist (INTP) or Catalyst (INFP)?

_____

_____

Which decision making function-attitude appears the best fit and why? Analyzing (Ti) or Valuing (Fi)?

_____

_____

What developmental factors might be relevant in selecting best-fit type?

_____

_____

8. DISTINGUISHING ISFP FROM INFP

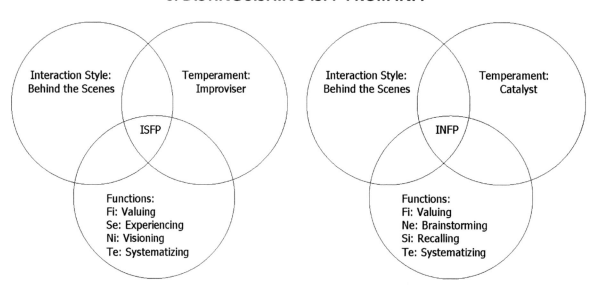

ISFPs and INFPs can look similar because they both tend to be quiet, supportive and caring. They both will tend to reflect before taking action as they have an **Introverting** preference, and may therefore show less obvious body language cues. They both make decisions using their Adult function: **Valuing (Fi).** This means that they are driven by strong internal beliefs, and push to align their external world with these internal values. They tend to be tolerant of differences, can be intensely private, and like to support others. Each type is strongly interested in people, although for different reasons. They both tend to use the **Behind the Scenes** Interaction Style which means that they prefer to integrate as much information as possible because they both believe it is worth the time investment to get the best result possible. They tend to believe that it's worth the time it takes to reconcile many inputs and they have a sense that if they keep gathering data, then they will be able to reconcile any inconsistencies. They tend to appear unassuming, approachable and friendly. Both types share the **Perceiving** preference and tend to view time as an elastic resource with the result that they tend to be flexible when situations change.

However, despite these similarities there are also a number of **marked differences** between ISFP's and INFPs. The following table highlights a few of these key indicators.

ISFP	INFP
Temperament	
ISFPs have the **Improviser** temperament. Improvisers need freedom, the ability to act in the moment and are able to enjoy the here and now. Improvisers tend to make the most of any situation and are talented at seizing current opportunities. Improvisers tend to read people well because they innately recognize what the other person wants from any given situation.	INFPs have the **Catalyst** temperament. Catalysts need a sense of purpose and meaning, the ability to help people develop their potential and are on a quest for identity. Catalysts tend to look for the best in any individuals they work with and are talented in seeing situations from the other person's perspectives. Catalysts tend to work well with individuals because they innately know what is important to the other person.
Stress Response Each stress response can cause the temperament to act diametrically differently from their innate abilities.	
Improvisers (ISFP) may deliberately miss deadlines or use deceptive agendas to cause a reaction when they are feeling confined or bored. The paradox of this stress response is to move from graceful to disgraceful.	Catalysts (INFP) may project negative attributions to others and use selective interpretation when they are feeling betrayed, or have to be insincere. The paradox of this stress response is to move from genuine to phony.

ISFP	INFP
Information Gathering Function-Attitudes	
ISFPs use **Experiencing (Se)**. They read all the concrete data in the moment – sound, sight, smell, taste, and touch. Using Experiencing (Se) in this way, will often mean they will pick up minute changes in facial expression, movements in body language, and comment on them. They are gifted at making ideas concrete and real.	**INFPs** use **Brainstorming (Ne)** and so tend to read between the lines and infer meaning from data. Using Brainstorming (Ne) in this way will often mean that they will make conclusions about people, but may not be able to give the specific source of the impressions. Their gift is in not being bounded by concrete reality, instead being able to explore possibilities without limit.

General Observations	
ISFPs tend to show an interest in practical reality and having fun with people, versus hypothesizing about behaviours. Their **concise, colourful** language will tend to get to the point quickly and will often be used to amuse colleagues and friends. Their literal communication style tends to "cut through" unnecessary detail.	**INFPs** enjoy learning about the theory of human behaviours, particularly in helping people get more out of life. Their **global, metaphorical** language will often include generalizations and talk about impressions versus specifics. Their more flowing style may appear to "meander" and include non-sequitors. This more abstract communication style can help to build bridges between apparently disparate points of view.

ISFP	INFP
General Observations	
ISFPs tend to use **Contextual Thinking** – the ability to respond in the moment to current stimuli. As a result they may miss implications from their actions. Although **ISFPs** have the **Perceiving** preference, they tend to naturally jump to decisions based on current data and are comfortable changing those decisions when new information becomes available.	**INFPs** tend to use **Integrative Thinking** – the ability to connect apparently disparate points of view. As a result they may appear to wander in their conversations. **INFPs** also share the **Perceiving** Preference. However they tend to naturally want to continue exploring possibilities and may postpone making a decision because this appears to close off other ideas.

Questions for sorting between Improviser and Catalyst temperaments

What drives you? What do you really enjoy doing? What was your best job?

- Listen for **Improviser's (ISFP)** drive for freedom, fun and seeing results in the moment, making an impact and being noticed.
- Listen for **Catalyst's (INFP)** drive for purpose, meaning and significance and to be seen as special.

What do you really struggle with? When was a time that you felt you had failed?

- Listen for **Improvisers (ISFP)** to describe long-term projects, with no tangible outcome, too many rules, boredom, and pointless details.
- Listen for **Catalysts (INFP)** to describe failure as being betrayed, being made to feel undervalued, or receiving no positive feedback, or lots of developmental feedback.

QUESTIONS FOR CLARIFYING TEMPERAMENT VIA CURRENT IMPACT OR FUTURE DIRECTION

Do you need to see immediate concrete results from your efforts?

- If **Yes,** consider **ISFP** because **Improvisers** tend to drive toward tangible results. ISFP's may also talk about getting an "aha" (as they access their Child Visioning Ni function) and then making it happen (supporting Experiencing Se as the Parent function).
- If **No,** consider **INFP** because **Catalysts** don't necessarily need to see a concrete outcome if they feel they have "touched" individuals and helped them get more out of their lives. Listen for past experiences (as they access their Child Recalling Si function) linked to exploring and inferring future potential with Brainstorming (Ne) as the Parent function.

Do you tend to focus on the here and now? Do you trust the future to take care of itself?
- If **Yes,** consider **Improviser (ISFP)** because Improvisers live in the present and seize the moment.
- If **No,** consider **Catalyst (INFP)** because Catalysts tend to be future-focused on their journey in support of their cause.

QUESTIONS TO IDENTIFY EXPERIENCING (SE) VERSUS BRAINSTORMING (NE)

Are you tuned in to physical changes of body language? Are you easily distracted by your environment? Do you like to see concrete results from your actions?
- If **Yes,** consider **Improviser (ISFP)** because Improvisers using **Experiencing (Se)** may tend to pick up changes in the external environment and enjoy making things real.
- If **No,** consider **Catalyst (INFP)** because Catalysts using **Brainstorming (Ne)** may tend to be more oblivious to physical clues as they focus on people's individuality, and concrete outcomes are less important.

8. Distinguishing ISFP from INFP: Review

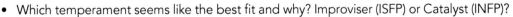

EXERCISE 15: DISTINGUISHING BETWEEN ISFP AND INFP
Thinking of these two personality types:
- Which temperament seems like the best fit and why? Improviser (ISFP) or Catalyst (INFP)?
- Which information gathering function-attitude appears the best fit and why? Experiencing (Se) or Brainstorming (Ne)?
- What developmental factors might be relevant in selecting best-fit type?

TRY IT ON!

DISTINGUISHING BETWEEN ISFP AND INFP

Which temperament seems like the best fit and why? Improviser (ISFP) or Catalyst (INFP?

_____

_____

Which information gathering function-attitude appears the best fit and why? Experiencing (Se) or Brainstorming (Ne)?

_____

_____

What developmental factors might be relevant in selecting best-fit type?

_____

_____

SUMMARY

As you can see, when individuals with an Introverting preference share three "letters" out of four, it can be tempting to see these types as similar.

However it is possible to have an in-depth exploration to ensure that the individual has correctly identified their best-fit type using the lenses of:

- Temperament
- Information Gathering Function-Attitudes
- Decision Making Function-Attitudes
- Hierarchy of Function-Attitudes
- Interaction Style

SCORECARD
- What did you learn from comparing similar Introverting type pairs?
- How will this approach help you in clarifying best-fit type?
- How else can you build your knowledge of the multiple lenses of type?

Chapter 5

Comparing Extraverting Type Pairs

GAME PLAN

In this section we will:

- Set the Scene
- Review pairs of Extraverting types as described below
- For each pair we will:
  - » Provide an overview of similarities
  - » Discuss differences in temperament, function-attitudes and Interaction Style (if relevant)
  - » Provide questions to help differentiate between two types
- Discuss key learning points

FOUL!

Remember as you read the descriptions, different types may demonstrate similar behaviours for different reasons. Always probe for Why an individual is acting in a specific way!

SET THE SCENE

This section has not been written to be read in sequence. Rather it has been written to reference as required depending on the person and the similar types that they are trying to understand more fully.

Each comparison of pairs has been written as a summary of key similarities and differences between the pairs of types listed below. Feel free to reference the introductory information at the beginning of the book, the type descriptions at the end of the book and the Resource Guide for further clarification on potential similarities and differences.

Good luck in your sorting process!

	ESTJ	ENTJ	ESFJ	ENFJ	ESTP	ENTP	ESFP
ENTJ	1						
ESFJ							
ENFJ		3	4				
ESTP	2						
ENTP					6		
ESFP			5				
ENFP						7	8

1. DISTINGUISHING ESTJ FROM ENTJ

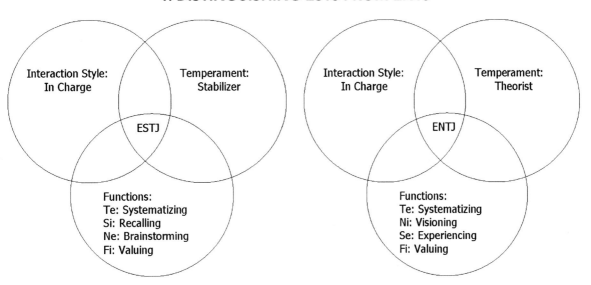

ESTJs and ENTJs share certain **core similarities**. Both have an **Extraverting** preference, so they tend to talk through action ideas and you may observe more expressive body language. Both tend to be action oriented, logical and quick to push for closure. Both types use the same function-attitude, **Systematizing (Te)** as their Adult function, to make objective decisions using causal-effect logic. Therefore both types can establish clear boundaries of "right" and 'wrong", are organized, systematic and methodical. Those who use Systematizing (Te) with ease are able to outline the steps required to make things happen, and structure people and resources to achieve the end goal in the most efficient way. In addition, both types use the **In Charge** Interaction Style: they are comfortable taking the first step in initiating relationships. They both tend to communicate their aims and goals clearly and are comfortable providing instructions and structure. They appear confident, commanding and straight-forward. They tend to be "social for a purpose": when there is no time pressure, or when the occasion demands, they may appear more like the Get Things Going style. When the time pressure is felt, the social element is submerged under the drive for action. Both will tend to make quick decisions and be comfortable taking, what other styles might perceive to be, risks.

However, there are also a number of **marked differences** between **ESTJs** and **ENTJs**:

ESTJ	ENTJ
Temperament	
ESTJs have a **Stabilizer** temperament. They need to be part of a team, and contribute to its concrete results. Stabilizers like to know their responsibilities, and they ensure that they live up to these demands. Then value security, stability and are economical with resources. They innately institute structure into chaos and create repeatable processes.	**ENTJs** have a **Theorist** temperament. They need to be knowledgeable and demonstrate competence in whatever ventures they deem important. Theorists like to view the world from a strategic perspective, with a constant eye to the future. They value autonomy and independence in their activities, and are constantly seeking new solutions. They employ intellectual rigour in their approach to facts and data.
Stress Response Each stress response can cause the temperament to act diametrically differently from their innate abilities.	
Stabilizers (ESTJ) may blame and complain when they are overloaded and others have not lived up to their responsibilities. The paradox of this stress response is to move from responsible to irresponsible.	**Theorists (ENTJ)** may become mentally paralysed when they perceive themselves to have been incompetent or they have lacked mastery. The paradox of this stress response is to move from rational to irrational.

ESTJ	ENTJ
Information Gathering Function-Attitudes	
ESTJs use **Recalling (Si)** as a Parent function. They perceive the current context, and then are able to refer back to their reference bank of stored sensory images, in order to compare and contrast the current data with previous experience. As this function works with their Adult function, **Systematizing (Te)**, it will help to ensure that action plans are grounded in reality to achieve the concrete goal.	**ENTJs** use **Visioning (Ni)** as a Parent function. They gather data and then need to step back to allow the information to incubate. After this time delay, the complete solution/idea appears, and it can appear very different from the original facts. As this function-attitude works with their Adult function, **Systematizing (Te)**, it will help to marshal necessary resources to achieve the vision in the most efficient way.
As **ESTJs** mature, you will see that they have greater access to their Child function **Brainstorming (Ne)** as they look at new possibilities that could be created based on their previous experience.	As **ENTJs** mature, you will see that they have greater access to their Child function **Experiencing (Se)** as they create ways to concretely express their vision using pictures, visuals or charts.

ESTJ	ENTJ
General Observations	
ESTJs tend to gravitate towards practical facts and data. Their **sequential, specific language** tends to layout the data in a step-by-step manner and may use words such as first, second, third with lots of examples. Their thorough communication style is excellent when providing instructions, putting a plan in place, or teaching others.	**ENTJs** tend to gravitate towards models, theories and concepts. Their **precise, accurate language** tends to constantly search for the correct word and may correct word choice to ensure that their understanding of the data is correct. Their enjoyment of debate, and ability to critical question the message in order to ensure multiple perspectives are considered, can help to dissect and clarify a point of view.
Other Observations	
ESTJs use the **Logistical Skill Set:** they are able to get the right things to the right place, in the right time frame – repeatedly. Their talent is to be able to organize and structure large amounts of logistics in an effortless manner. **ESTJs** use **Sequential Thinking:** the ability to naturally put first things first.	**ENTJs** use **the Strategic Skill Set:** they are able to assess the relationships between the means and the ends, and take a long-term strategic view. Their talent is to be able to identify innovative ways to make progress towards long-term goals. **ENTJs** use **Differential Thinking:** the ability to naturally see the distinctions between things.

QUESTIONS FOR SORTING BETWEEN STABILIZER AND THEORIST

What drives you? What do you really enjoy doing?

- Listen for the **Stabilizer's (ESTJ)** drive for team membership, producing concrete results, and being responsible.
- Listen for the **Theorist's (ENTJ)** drive for competence, autonomy, and being knowledgeable.

What do you really struggle with? When was a time that you felt you had failed?

- Listen for **Stabilizers (ESTJ)** to describe projects with constant change, no structure and no team support.
- Listen for **Theorists (ENTJ)** to describe situations with no ability to influence future outcomes, overloaded with details, and failure in more than two areas.

QUESTIONS FOR CLARIFYING TEMPERAMENT VIA IMPROVEMENT OR REDESIGN

Is your drive to improve a system paramount and do you often search for a completely innovative system to accomplish the goal?

- If **Yes**, consider **ENTJ**, because **Theorists** employ double-loop problem solving: they will look outside the current system for innovative solutions.
- If **No**, consider **ESTJ**, because **Stabilizers** like to improve within the current context to improve efficiency and will only reluctantly discard the current structure.

Do you tend to focus on involving people in accomplishing results?

- If **Yes**, consider **ESTJ**, because **Stabilizers** are one of the collaborative temperaments and innately want to build involvement from people.
- If **No**, consider **ENTJ**, as **Theorists** are one of the pragmatic temperaments, who tend to focus on doing what it takes to accomplish the task.

QUESTIONS FOR SORTING BETWEEN RECALLING (SI) AND VISIONING (NI) FUNCTION-ATTITUDES

When you begin a project, do you automatically think back to what you did before, what worked?

- If **Yes**, consider **ESTJ**, because **Stabilizers** using **Recalling (Si)** tend to begin with historic data, and as a result are able to articulate what is real and practical.
- If **No**, consider **ENTJ**, because **Theorists** using **Visioning (Ni)** may be unable to access past experience, as their energy is focused on future models and plans.

QUESTIONS FOR SORTING BETWEEN WHY AND HOW?

When beginning a project, is the What and Why of the project important to you?

- If **Yes**, consider **ENTJ**, because **Theorists** will tend to see **What** the long-term goal is and **Why** they are trying to accomplish it. The steps on How to achieve this are secondary.
- If **No**, consider **ESTJ** because **Stabilizers** will tend to see **What** the goal is and focus on **How** to achieve this.

1. Distinguishing ESTJ and ENTJ: Review

EXERCISE 16: DISTINGUISHING BETWEEN ESTJ AND ENTJ

Thinking of these two personality types:
- Which temperament seems like the best fit and why? Stabilizer (ESTJ) or Theorist (ENTJ)?
- Which information gathering function-attitude appears the best fit and why? Recalling (Si) or Visioning (Ni)?
- What developmental factors might be relevant in selecting best-fit type?

TRY IT ON!

DISTINGUISHING BETWEEN ESTJ AND ENTJ

Which temperament seems like the best fit and why? Stabilizer (ESTJ) or Theorist (ENTJ)?

_____

_____

Which information gathering function-attitude appears the best fit and why? Recalling (Si) or Visioning (Ni)?

_____

_____

What developmental factors might be relevant in selecting best-fit type?

_____

_____

2. DISTINGUISHING ESTJ FROM ESTP

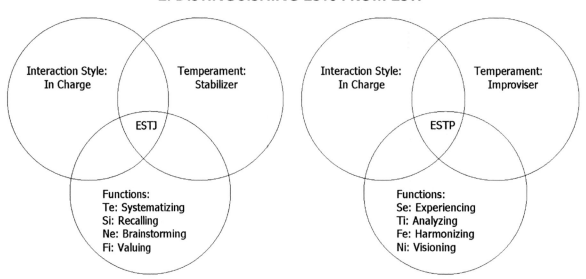

ESTJs and ESTPs share many **core similarities**. Both types share an **Extraverting** preference so their energy cycles out first to the world of people and things for action and discussion, before cycling in for reflection. Both tend to be practical, hands-on, logical and quick to push for closure. Both use the **Sensing** preference so start with the details to build to the big picture, and enjoy achieving tangible results. They both tend to use concrete language in expressing themselves with examples, stories, and specifics. Both types use the **In Charge** Interaction Style and are comfortable taking the first step in initiating relationships. They naturally are more comfortable giving directions, providing guidance and stating instructions. They tend to make quick and expedient decisions as they drive towards an achievable result. They like to move quickly towards a goal and are willing to take a risk in order to decide. They can be frustrated if they do not see action. They both enjoy controlling the assets required to reach a goal whether they be people or resources. They both have a fast-paced, determined energy and appear confident and straightforward. Both types share the **Thinking** preference and tend to focus on truth, facts, logic and underlying principles.

However, there are also a number of **significant differences** between **ESTJs** and **ESTPs**:

ESTJ	ESTP
Temperament	
ESTJs have a **Stabilizer** temperament. Stabilizers need to be part of a team, and contribute to its concrete results. They like to know their responsibilities, and they ensure that they live up to these demands. They value security, stability and are economical with resources.	**ESTPs** have an **Improviser** temperament. Improvisers need freedom, the ability to act in the moment, and enjoy seeing immediate tangible results. They like to make the most of any situation and are talented at present-focused tactics. They value excitement, variety and have an innate aesthetic awareness.
Stress Response Each stress response can cause the temperament to act diametrically differently from their innate abilities.	
Stabilizers (ESTJ) may nag and try to control others by telling what has to be done by when and how. The paradox of this stress response is to move from responsible to irresponsible.	**Improvisers (ESTP)** may behave outrageously or stir things up in order to cause a reaction. The paradox of this stress response is to move from graceful to disgraceful.

ESTJ	ESTP
Information Gathering Function-attitudes	
ESTJs primarily use **Recalling (Si)** to gather data. They perceive the current context, and then are able to refer back to their large databank of stored sensory images, in order to compare and contrast the current data with previous experience. As such, they will be able to bring the best of the past to the future, enable others to learn from mistakes and can provide the "group memory."	**ESTPs** primarily use **Experiencing (Se)** to gather data. They perceive all the concrete data in the moment – sound, sight, smell, taste, and touch in order to fully experience the here and now. As such they are tuned in to the current context, are fully ware of all that is currently happening and this can enable them to seize opportunities and suggest creative options in the moment.
Decision Making Function-Attitudes	
ESTJs primarily use **Systematizing (Te)** to make objective decisions using causal-effect logic. They can establish clear boundaries of "right" and 'wrong", are organized and methodical. Those who use Systematizing (Te) with ease are able to outline the steps required to make things happen, and structure people and resources to achieve the end goal in the most efficient way.	**ESTPs** primarily use **Analyzing (Ti)** to make decisions by dissecting and categorizing data, evaluating it against internal criteria, and making independent decisions using this mental model. They can create new logical frameworks and reframe situations. Those who use Analyzing (Ti) with ease excel at examining an argument, creating a unique point of view, and approaching problems using root cause analysis.

ESTJ	ESTP
General Observations	
ESTJs tend to use **sequential, specific language** in order to layout the data in a step-by-step manner, with lots of examples. Their thorough communication style is excellent when providing instructions, putting a plan in place, or teaching others.	ESTPs tend to use **concise, colourful language** in order to get to the point quickly. The KISS philosophy: Keep It Short and Simple! Their brief communication style is effective when time is of the essence, and key messages need to be communicated in the most efficient and clear way.
Adult Function	
The Adult Function for **ESTJs** is **Systematizing (Te)** (a Judging function-attitude) which means that there is a push to make decisions and stick with them.	The Adult Function for **ESTPs** is **Experiencing (Se)** (a Perceiving function-attitude) which means that there is an openness to changing decisions as new information becomes available.

QUESTIONS FOR SORTING BETWEEN STABILIZER AND IMPROVISER TEMPERAMENTS

What drives you? What do you really enjoy doing?

- Listen for the **Stabilizer's (ESTJ)** drive for team membership, producing results, loyalty and being responsible.
- Listen for the **Improviser's (ESTP)** drive for freedom, fun, making an impact and being noticed.

What do you really struggle with? When was a time that you felt you had failed?

- Listen for **Stabilizers (ESTJ)** to describe projects with constant change, no structure and no team support.
- Listen for **Improvisers (ESTP)** to describe long-term projects, with no tangible outcome, too many rules, and pointless details

Do you innately institute structure in order to achieve the goal in the most efficient, consistent manner?

- If **Yes**, consider **ESTJ**, because **Stabilizers** tend to instinctively institute processes and procedures to manage logistical details in the most ordered way.
- If **No**, consider **ESTP**, because **Improvisers** tend to rely on the ability to respond to the current context without rules and structure in order to achieve the most expedient solution.

Do you tend to focus on how actions might affect the team performance?
- If **Yes**, consider **ESTJ**, because **Stabilizers** are one of the collaborative temperaments and tend to focus more on interdependence and cooperative interactions.
- If **No**, consider **ESTP**, as **Improvisers** are one of the pragmatic temperaments and tend to focus more on independence and autonomous actions.

When you are starting a new project, do you tend to go back to what you did last time, so that you can compare and contrast what worked then?

- If **Yes**, consider **Stabilizer (ESTJ)**, because Stabilizers, using **Recalling (Si)**, will normally track back in time to think about what was done in what sequence, and then think about how it could be applied in the current context.
- If **No**, consider **Improviser (ESTP)**, because Improvisers using **Experiencing (Se)** tend to jump in and focus more on the here and now, with less focus on past data.

When you have to make a decision, do you like to put a plan in place and stick to the plan?

- If **Yes**, consider **ESTJ**, because **Stabilizers** using **Systematizing (Te)** tend to push for decisions using external facts and logical data, and like to stick to a plan and execute it once it is made.
- If **No**, consider **ESTP** because **Improvisers** using **Analyzing (Ti)** may prefer to dissect data, argue their point of view, and change their decisions as additional information becomes available.

2. Distinguishing ESTJ from ESTP: Review

EXERCISE 17: DISTINGUISHING BETWEEN ESTJ AND ESTP

Thinking of these two personality types:

- Which temperament seems like the best fit and why? Stabilizer (ESTJ) or Improviser (ESTP)?
- Which information gathering function-attitude appears the best fit and why? Recalling (Si) or Experiencing (Se)?
- Which decision making function-attitude appears the best fit and why? Systematizing (Te) or Analyzing (Ti)?
- What developmental factors might be relevant in selecting best-fit type?

TRY IT ON!

DISTINGUISHING BETWEEN ESTJ AND ESTP

Which temperament seems like the best fit and why? Stabilizer (ESTJ) or Improviser (ESTP)?

_____

_____

Which information gathering function-attitude appears the best fit and why? Recalling (Si) or Experiencing (Se)?

_____

_____

Which decision making function-attitude appears the best fit and why? Systematizing (Te) or Analyzing (Ti)?

_____

_____

What developmental factors might be relevant in selecting best-fit type?

_____

_____

3. DISTINGUISHING ENFJ FROM ENTJ

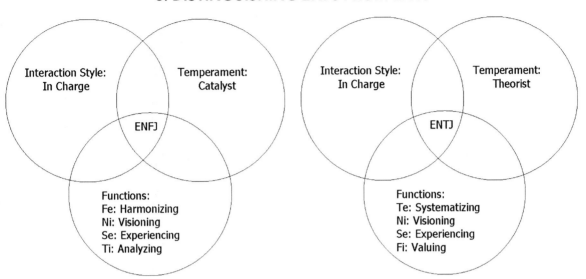

ENFJs and ENTJs share certain **core similarities.** They naturally try to affect the world around them using **the In Charge** Interaction Style. They share the core belief that it is worth the risk to take action or make a decision in order to meet their drive to accomplish results. They both tend to communicate with a time and task focus, and take the first move in initiating relationships. Both share the In Charge confident and energetic style. Both types gather information using **Visioning (Ni),** which means that they tend to collect data and then unconsciously step back to allow the information to incubate. After this time delay, the complete solution/idea appears, and it can appear very different from the original facts. This function-attitude is able to simplify the complex, and unify different approaches. Both types share the **iNtuiting** preference and in communicating they both tend to use more abstract language: talking about concepts and ideas, making inferences and using more theoretical terms rather than providing specific examples. In addition both types share an **Extraverting** preference so their energy flows outwards to the world of people and things, which can mean that they are more verbally expressive, use more gestures and talk things through rather than think things through. Finally both types share the **Judging** preference in which they use their decision making function-attitude in the external world and therefore tend to push for closure and prefer to have a plan in place.

However, there are also a number of marked **differences** between ENFJs and ENTJs:

ENFJ	ENTJ
Temperament	
ENFJs have a **Catalyst** temperament. Catalysts need to have a unique identity and have a sense of meaning in the work that they do. They value empathic relationships in their lives and support cooperative interaction when engaging with others. Catalysts possess the **diplomatic skill set** which is able to unify different points of view by understanding and resolving deeper issues, and use metaphors and analogies to communicate meaning. Catalysts are one of the two collaborative temperaments (with Stabilizers) valuing inclusion and interdependence.	**ENTJs** have a **Theorist** temperament. Theorists need to be knowledgeable and demonstrate competence in whatever ventures they deem important. They value autonomy and control in their activities, and employ intellectual rigor in their approach to facts and data. Theorists possess the **strategic skill set** which is able to view information from an abstract perspective, analyze the connections between goals and means and identify ways to achieve the goal. Theorists are one of the two pragmatic temperaments (with Improvisers) valuing self-determination and independence.
Stress Response Each stress response can cause the temperament to act diametrically differently from their innate abilities.	
Catalysts may emotionally disconnect and over-generalize a negative situation. The paradox of this stress response is that they move from genuine to phony.	**Theorists** may become mentally paralyzed when they perceive themselves to have been incompetent. The paradox of this stress response is to move from rational to irrational.

ENFJ	ENTJ
Decision Making Function-Attitudes	
ENFJs use Adult **Harmonizing (Fe)** to make subjective decisions to structure the external world. They therefore tend to be empathetic and people-focused. They like to make decisions to achieve consensus and are gifted at creating a safe environment. Using Harmonizing (Fe) with ease, they are adept at self-disclosing to connect with others, and excel at initiating, building and maintaining personal relationships.	**ENTJs** use Adult **Systematizing (Te)** to make objective decisions to structure the external world. They therefore tend to be organized and methodical. They like to make decisions using causal effect logic and are gifted in defining clear boundaries in the work and home context. Using Systematizing (Te) with ease, they are adept at outlining the steps required to make things happen, and excel at structuring people and resources to achieve the end goal in the most efficient way.

General Observations	
ENFJs tend to use **global language** when communicating as they use **integrative thinking** to connect seemingly diverse points of view. This global language will often include generalizations and talk about impressions versus specifics. Their more flowing style may appear to meander and to include non-sequiturs as they "connect the dots."	**ENTJs** tend to use **precise language** when communicating as they use **differential** thinking to analyze, dissect and refine concepts and ideas. This precise language will often include critical questioning to clarify understanding and thought process. Their debating style may also include correcting other people's word choice to ensure accuracy of their perception.

QUESTIONS FOR SORTING BETWEEN CATALYST AND THEORIST TEMPERAMENTS

What drives you? What do you really enjoy doing?
- Listen for the **Catalyst's (ENFJ)** drive for purpose, significance and to be seen as special.
- Listen for the **Theorist's (ENTJ)** drive for knowledge, competence and to be seen as an expert.

What do you really struggle with? When was a time that you felt you had failed?
- Listen for **Catalysts (ENFJ)** to describe failure as being betrayed, being made to feel undervalued, receiving no positive feedback, or lots of developmental feedback.
- Listen for **Theorists (ENTJ)** to describe failure as having no ability to influence future outcomes, overloaded with details, no big picture and being perceived to be incompetent.

Do you tend to focus on logically improving an overall system to achieve a goal?
- If **No** consider **ENFJ**, because **Catalysts** tend to focus more on developing people in their quest to achieve an idealised and meaningful world.
- If **Yes** consider **ENTJ**, because **Theorists** employ double-loop problem solving: they will look outside the current system in their quest for ultimate truths or theories.

QUESTIONS FOR CLARIFYING FUNCTION-ATTITUDES

Do you value logic over emotion?
- If **No** consider **Catalyst (ENFJ)**, because Catalysts, using **Harmonizing (Fe)** prefer to consider first the people, their values and what is appropriate in a situation.
- If **Yes** consider **Theorist (ENTJ)**, because Theorists using **Systematizing (Te)** prefer to consider first the logical sequence of events and what is efficient in a situation.

If you are faced with a personal conflict, are you comfortable in taking the steps necessary to resolve the conflict in order to move on in a productive manner?

- If **No**, consider **Catalyst (ENFJ)**, because Catalysts, using **Harmonizing (Fe)** tend to want to avoid loss of personal relationship through disharmony and may therefore avoid dealing with the conflict.
- If **Yes**, consider **Theorist (ENTJ)**, because Theorists using **Systematizing (Te)** tend to focus on objective data and therefore are more comfortable in addressing conflict so as to move on with the matters at hand.

3. Distinguishing ENFJ from ENTJ: Review

EXERCISE 18: DISTINGUISHING BETWEEN ENFJ AND ENTJ

Thinking of these two personality types:

- Which temperament seems like the best fit and why? Catalyst (ENFJ) or Theorist (ENTJ)?
- Which decision making function-attitude appears the best fit and why? Harmonizing (Fe) or Systematizing (Te)?
- What developmental factors might be relevant in selecting best-fit type?

TRY IT ON!

DISTINGUISHING BETWEEN ENFJ AND ENTJ

Which temperament seems like the best fit and why? Catalyst (ENFJ) or Theorist (ENTJ)?

_____

_____

Which decision making function-attitude appears the best fit and why? Harmonizing (Fe) or Systematizing (Te)?

_____

_____

What developmental factors might be relevant in selecting best-fit type?

_____

_____

4. DISTINGUISHING ESFJ FROM ENFJ

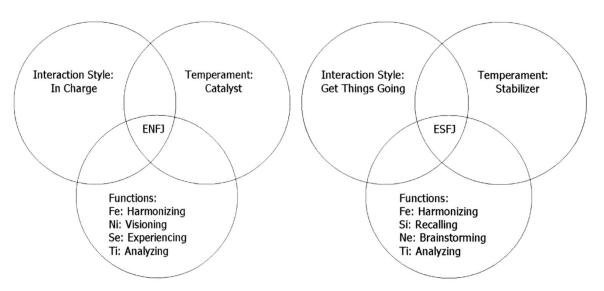

There are a number of **core similarities** between those with a preference for **ESFJ** and those with a preference for **ENFJ**. Both types share Adult **Harmonizing (Fe)**, so their leading function drives them to make decisions in the external world to optimize interpersonal harmony. As a result, they can look similar because they both tend to be empathetic, people-focused and organized. Both types like to achieve consensus and are gifted at creating a safe environment. Using Harmonizing (Fe), they are adept at self-disclosing to connect with others, may show their emotions on their face (on good and bad days!), and may struggle when there is an extreme conflict. They share an innate knowledge of what is appropriate in any given situation and others will feel welcomed and supported in an interaction. Both types share an **Extraverting** preference which means that they tend to talk through their ideas with others, and communicate with enthusiasm using more expressive body language. They both use an internal information gathering function-attitude, so will go inwards for new data before making decisions externally. Finally, they both share the **Judging** preference so they tend to push for closure in the external world, and will enjoy planning for future outcomes. They like to set goals and push to achieve them on time, and tend to view time as a finite resource to be budgeted.

Despite these **similarities**, however, there are also a number of **marked differences** between **ESFJs** and **ENFJs**. The following table highlights a few of these key indicators.

ESFJ	ENFJ
Temperament	
ESFJs have a **Stabilizer** temperament. Stabilizers need to know what they are responsible for, and like to live up to these responsibilities. They tend to enjoy being part of a team, and enjoy contributing to concrete goal accomplishment. Stabilizers tend to be collaborative with other teammates, and enjoy instituting processes to build structure and stability.	**ENFJs** have a **Catalyst** temperament. Catalysts need a sense of purpose and meaning, and like to work with a cause. They are passionate about helping people develop their potential, and are on a constant quest for identity. Catalysts tend to work well with individuals, as they use empathy to put themselves in the other person's shoes.
Stress Response Each stress response can cause the temperament to act diametrically differently from their innate abilities.	
Stabilizers (ESFJ) may become worried and depressed when they feel they have been pushed too far. The paradox of this stress response is that they move from responsible to irresponsible.	**Catalysts (ENFJ)** may sacrifice their own identities to be the person someone else wants them to be, when they have no purpose. The paradox of this stress response is that they move from genuine to phony.

ESFJ	ENFJ
Information Gathering Function-Attitudes	
ESFJs use **Recalling (Si).** When required to begin a new activity, they tend to go back in time, to think of what worked and what didn't work, and look at what they would do differently this time. Using Recalling (Si) in this way often means they have a clear sense of what is real or practical in any given situation. As they mature ESFJs will more obviously use their Child **Brainstorming (Ne)** function-attitude to see patterns and possibilities building on their sense of concrete reality. In this way, they may start to identify with the iNtuiting preference.	**ENFJs** use **Visioning (Ni).** When required to begin a new activity, they tend to gather data and unconsciously connect this information into a new idea or picture. Using Visioning (Ni) in this way will often mean that they need to step back and allow ideas to 'gel', and the final picture may be very different from the original information. As they mature ENFJs will more obviously use their Child **Experiencing (Se)** function to tune into the current reality and make their insights more concrete. In this way, they may start to identify with the Sensing preference.

ESFJ	ENFJ
Interaction Style	
ESFJs use the **Get Things Going** Interaction Style. This means that they tend to believe it is worth the time it takes to engage others. Their energy tends to be expressive and they can be stressed by not being involved or left out. They excel at organizing tasks to make life easier.	ENFJs use the **In Charge** Interaction Style This means that they tend to believe it is worth taking a risk to decide and correcting later. Their energy tends to be determined and they can be stressed by the appearance of nothing happening. They excel at mentoring individuals towards development goals.
General Observations	
ESFJs tend to want any theories to result in practical application, and normally provide examples when talking. Their **sequential communication style** will often include a beginning, middle and end, with a step-by-step pacing. Common words and expressions include 'in my experience', 'in the past', etc.	ENFJs enjoy learning the theory of human behaviours, particularly in helping people develop their potential. Their **global language** will often include generalisations and talk about impressions versus specifics. Their more flowing style may appear to meander and to include such words as always, never, etc.

QUESTIONS FOR SORTING BETWEEN CATALYST AND THEORIST TEMPERAMENTS

What drives you? What do you really enjoy doing?
- Listen for the Stabilizer's (ESFJ) drive for responsibility, membership, belonging to the team, and concrete goal achievement.
- Listen for the Catalyst's (ENFJ) drive for purpose, meaning, and to be seen as special.

What do you really struggle with? When was a time that you felt you had failed?
- Listen for **Stabilizers (ESFJ)** to describe projects where no one lived up to their responsibilities, where there was constant change and no sense of teamwork.
- Listen for **Catalysts (ENFJ)** to describe failure as being betrayed, being made to feel undervalued, receiving no positive feedback, or lots of developmental feedback.

Do you like theories pertaining to people only if there is a practical application?
- If **Yes**, consider **ESFJ**, because **Stabilizers** tend to enjoy focusing on people, if there is some explicit, useful result.

- If **No**, consider **ENFJ**, because **Catalysts** don't necessarily need to see a concrete outcome if they feel they have 'touched' individuals and helped them get more out of their lives. They tend to imply the results.

Do you tend to be more risk averse? Do you tend to put in contingency plans to protect against things going wrong?

- If **Yes**, consider **Stabilizer (ESFJ)**, because Stabilizers tend to be more cautious, and are adept at planning for things that might go wrong.
- If **No**, consider **Catalyst (ENFJ)**, because Catalysts, with their natural optimism, tend to take more risks without necessarily considering possible challenges.

QUESTIONS FOR CLARIFYING FUNCTION-ATTITUDES

When you are starting a new project, do you tend to go back to what you did last time, so that you can compare and contrast what worked then?

- If **Yes** consider **Stabilizer (ESFJ)**, because Stabilizers, using **Recalling (Si)**, will track back in time to compare and contrast the current project with past workload. For this reason, Stabilizers may struggle with completing a task they have not undertaken before.
- If **No**, consider **Catalyst (ENFJ)**, because Catalysts using **Visioning (Ni)** tend to be more future focused as they create their own "picture" of the future. For this reason, they may forget to refer back to past experience and learn from mistakes.

QUESTIONS FOR CLARIFYING INTERACTION STYLE

When you are working on a project and there is a fixed time frame, do you tend to drive through to conclusion with the risk that occasionally you alienate the people?

- If **Yes** consider **In Charge Catalyst (ENFJ)**, because ENFJs, with the drive for action may become too directing and forget the people component.
- If **No**, consider **Get Things Going Stabilizer (ESFJ)**, because ESFJs, with the drive to involve others would tend to focus on the people and process first and the task second.

4. Distinguishing ESFJ from ENFJ: Review

EXERCISE 19: DISTINGUISHING BETWEEN ESFJ AND ENFJ

Thinking of these two personality types:

- Which temperament seems like the best fit and why? Stabilizer (ESFJ) or Catalyst (ENFJ)?
- Which information gathering function-attitude appears to be the best fit and why? Recalling (Si) or Visioning (Ni)?
- Which Interaction Style seems the best fit and why? Get Things Going or In Charge?
- What developmental factors might be relevant in selecting best-fit type?

TRY IT ON!

DISTINGUISHING BETWEEN ESFJ AND ENFJ

Which temperament seems like the best fit and why? Stabilizer (ESFJ) or Catalyst (ENFJ)?

_____

_____

Which information gathering function-attitude appears to be the best fit and why? Recalling (Si) or Visioning (Ni)?

_____

_____

Which Interaction Style seems the best fit and why? Get Things Going or In Charge?

_____

_____

What developmental factors might be relevant in selecting best-fit type?

_____

_____

5. DISTINGUISHING ESFJ FROM ESFP

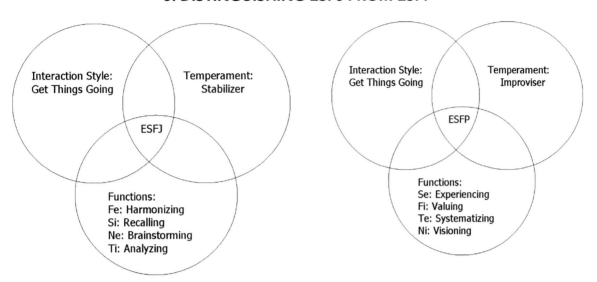

ESFJs and ESFPs share certain **core similarities**. Both use the **Get Things Going** Interaction Style, which means that they tend to naturally make collaborative decisions to involve others and achieve buy-in. They innately focus on motivating others and raising commitment, and believe it is worth the time spent to engage others. They both tend to project an enthusiastic and welcoming energy, and tend to get stressed when they are not included in discussions. They both are comfortable making the first move in relationships (Initiating) and may think out loud and jump in with comments. They also both use a more Informing style of communication, which involves giving information and allowing people to make their own decision, rather than telling them what to do. Both types share the **Extraverting** preference and so they may tend to act first and reflect later. Both have a **Sensing** preference and tend to use more concrete, literal language, giving examples, specifics or stories. They both tend to be more practical, and trust what they observe currently, or what they have experienced in the past. They both have a **Feeling** preference and tend to make decisions using qualitative data. Both types will appear to be hands-on, energetic and fun.

Despite these core similarities, however, there are also a number of **marked differences** between **ESFJs** and **ESFPs.**

ESFJ	ESFP
Temperament	
ESFJs have a Stabilizer temperament. They need to know what they are responsible for, and like to live up to those responsibilities. Stabilizers enjoy being part of a team and contributing to the accomplishment of concrete goals. They tend to be collaborative with team mates, and enjoy instituting processes to build structure and stability.	ESFPs have an Improviser temperament. They need to make an impact and be noticed in their activities. Improvisers enjoy the freedom to act in the moment and being impressive. They tend to be pragmatic (doing what it takes to achieve the goals), and enjoy flexibility and variety in their daily work.
Stress Response Each stress response can cause the temperament to act diametrically differently from their innate abilities.	
Stabilizers (ESFJ) may get worried and depressed when others do not live up to their responsibilities. The paradox of this stress response is that they move from responsible to irresponsible.	Improvisers (ESFP) may leave projects to the last minute or forget them all together when they feel confined or bored. The paradox of this stress response is that they move from graceful to disgraceful.

ESFJ	ESFP
Information Gathering Function-Attitudes	
ESFJs use Recalling (Si) to gather data. When required to begin a new activity, they tend to go back in time to think of what worked and what didn't work, and look at what they would do differently this time. Using Recalling (Si) in this way often means they have a clear sense of what is real or practical in any situation, although that can also manifest itself in appearing negative: "that did not work before."	ESFPs use Experiencing (Se) to gather data. When required to begin a new activity, they tend to focus on current sensory information: what is actually happening, and what immediate options this data can provide. Using Experiencing (Se) in this way often means they are able to seize opportunities, although they may be so absorbed in the current reality that they miss reading between the lines.
Decision Making Function-Attitudes	
ESFJs use Harmonizing (Fe) to make decisions. Harmonizing involves making decisions to optimize interpersonal harmony. Those using this function-attitude are often gifted at creating a safe environment where others can express opinions. Using Harmonizing with ease, ESFJs tend to be comfortable self-disclosing to connect, and are more likely to push for consensus.	ESFPs use Valuing (Fi) to make decisions. Valuing involves making subjective decisions using an internal belief system. Those using this function-attitude are often tolerant, non-intrusive and supportive of individual differences. Using Valuing with ease, ESFPs tend to be private in sharing their inner thoughts, and are driven to live life in alignment with their own internal values.

ESFJ	ESFP
General Observations	
ESFJ's Adult function is **Harmonizing (Fe)** supported by **Recalling (Si)**. This means that they tend to push for closure in the external world and gather information internally. They will naturally prefer knowing what to expect and will build a plan and stick to it. Their **sequential detailed language** will often include a beginning, middle and end, with a step-by-step pacing. Common words and expressions include 'in my experience', 'in the past', etc.	**ESFP's** Adult function is **Experiencing (Se)** supported by **Valuing (Fi)**. This means that they are constantly open to new ideas in the external world, with an internal decision-making process. They will naturally either not make a plan, or make a plan and change it or ignore it, as they respond to the here and now. Their **concise, informal language** will often include jargon, colloquialisms, and a focus on 'Keep It Short and Simple'. Their to-the-point style will tend to include words such as "it depends on the situation", "I can adapt in the moment."

QUESTIONS FOR SORTING BETWEEN STABILIZER AND IMPROVISER TEMPERAMENTS

What drives you? What do you really enjoy doing?

- Listen for the **Stabilizer's (ESFJ)** drive for responsibility, membership, belonging to the team, and concrete goal achievement.
- Listen for the **Improviser's (ESFP)** drive for freedom, fun, and seeing immediate, concrete results.

What do you really struggle with? When was a time you felt you have failed?

- Listen for **Stabilizers (ESFJ)** to describe projects where no one lived up to their responsibilities, where there was constant, pointless change, no sense of teamwork.
- Listen for **Improvisers (ESFP)** to describe long-term projects, with no tangible outcome, too many rules, and pointless boring details.

How do you feel about rules? Do you accept them?

- If **Yes** consider **ESFJ** because **Stabilizers** tend to institute rules and guidelines in order to achieve consistency and ensure repeatable processes.
- If **No** consider **ESFP** because **Improvisers** tend to avoid, ignore or work around rules, as they view these as inhibiting their ability to make choices based on the current context.

Do you tend to be risk-averse? Do you tend to put in contingency plans to protect against things going wrong?

- If **Yes**, consider **ESFJ** because **Stabilizers** tend to be more cautious, and are adept at planning for things that might go wrong.
- If **No**, consider **ESFP** because **Improvisers**, with their sensory acuity, tend to believe that whatever goes wrong, they will be able to respond to it.

QUESTIONS FOR CLARIFYING INFORMATION GATHERING FUNCTION-ATTITUDES

Are you tuned in to physical changes of body language? Are you easily distracted by physical factors in your environment?

- If **No**, consider **ESFJ** because **Stabilizers**, using **Recalling (Si)**, tend to take the current data, and then their energy moves inside as they compare this data with their rich databank of sensory experiences. As a result, they might not be distracted by external factors.
- If **Yes**, consider **ESFP** because **Improvisers**, using **Experiencing (Se)**, tend to concentrate on changes in the external environment, and may be distracted by physical concrete data as they are continually searching out external sensory data.

QUESTIONS FOR CLARIFYING DECISION MAKING FUNCTION-ATTITUDES

If necessary, are you willing to engage in tough discussions in order to achieve the 'right' decisions?

- If **No**, consider **ESFJ** because **Stabilizers**, using **Harmonizing (Fe)**, normally try to avoid conflict and work to gain agreement. Achieving the best overall decision will often take precedence over adhering to individual beliefs.
- If **Yes**, consider **ESFP** because **Improvisers**, using **Valuing (Fi)**, can be easygoing and people-focused, but will often stand up strongly if a decision is not in alignment with their internal values framework.

5. Distinguishing ESFJ from ESFP: Review

EXERCISE 20: DISTINGUISHING BETWEEN ESFJ AND ESFP

Thinking of these two personality types:

- Which temperament seems like the best fit and why? Stabilizer (ESFJ) or Improviser (ESFP)?
- Which information gathering function-attitude appears to be the best fit and why? Recalling (Si) or Experiencing (Se)?
- Which decision making function-attitude appears to be the best fit and why? Harmonizing (Fe) or Valuing (Fi)?
- What developmental factors might be relevant in selecting best-fit type?

TRY IT ON!

DISTINGUISHING BETWEEN ESFJ AND ESFP

Which temperament seems like the best fit and why? Stabilizer (ESFJ) or Improviser (ESFP)?

_____

_____

Which information gathering function-attitude appears to be the best fit and why? Recalling (Si) or Experiencing (Se)?

_____

_____

Which decision making function-attitude appears to be the best fit and why? Harmonizing (Fe) or Valuing (Fi)?

_____

_____

What developmental factors might be relevant in selecting best-fit type?

_____

_____

6. DISTINGUISHING ESTP FROM ENTP

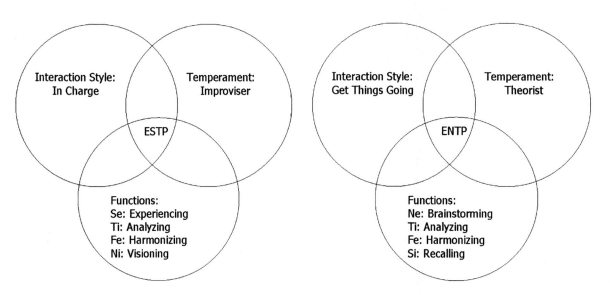

ESTPs and **ENTPs** share certain **core similarities** because they both tend to be energetic, competitive, and adaptable. Both types share the **Extraverting** preference so their energy cycles out first to the external world of people and events, before going inside for reflection. As a result, both types may tend to use more expressive body language and have a greater diversity of relationships. Both types gather information externally and see options and opportunities. With that information, they make decisions using the same Parent function: **Analyzing (Ti)**. Analyzing involves gathering logical data and evaluating it against internal criteria. Those who use Analyzing (Ti) with ease excel at dissecting an argument, creating a unique point of view, and approaching problems from various logical perspectives. Both types may tend to ask critical questions to clarify reasoning and may resist new rationales if they do not mesh with their personal mental model. Both tend to be pragmatic, recognizing the need to do what it takes to accomplish the goal. Both types share the **Perceiving** preference so they both tend to view time as a renewable resource, and will be comfortable changing decisions if circumstances change.

However, despite these similarities there are also a number of **marked differences** between **ESTPs** and **ENTPs**:

ESTP	ENTP
Temperament	
ESTPs have an **Improviser** temperament. Improvisers need freedom, the ability to act in the moment, and enjoy the here and now. Improvisers tend to make the most of any situation and are talented at implementing present-focused tactics.	**ENTPs** have a **Theorist** temperament. Theorists need knowledge, competence, and a degree of autonomy and control over their own destiny. Theorists tend to be future-focused and are talented at seeing things from a strategic, long-term perspective.
Stress Response Each stress response can cause the temperament to act diametrically differently from their innate abilities.	
Improvisers may escalate the situation and take action to cause a reaction such as using off-colour humour or not doing what they say they will do. Their stress motto could be, "Love me, hate me, but don't ignore or bore me!"	**Theorists** may become preoccupied and appear emotionally distant as they pull back internally to focus on their perceived failure. Their stress motto could be, "If I had only said or done this, I would have been masterful!"
ESTP	ENTP
Information Gathering Functions	
ESTPs use **Experiencing (Se)** to gather data from the external world. They naturally live in a physical world where they are able to read all the concrete data in the moment – sound, sight, smell, taste, and touch. This enables them to be creative at seeing concrete options and seizing immediate opportunities.	**ENTPs** use **Brainstorming (Ne)** to gather data from the external world. They naturally live in a world of ideas where they are able to see connections and meanings, and abstract patterns and possibilities. This enables them to be creative at reading between the lines and suggesting how things could be made better.
Interaction Style	
ESTPs use the **In Charge** Interaction Style which means that they innately focus on the immediate environment, executing tasks and removing obstacles. Their energy tends to be fast-paced, confident and determined. They tend to focus on the tools at hand to solve immediate problems and get results.	**ENTPs** use the **Get Things Going** Interaction Style which means that they innately focus on involving others in exploring ideas and sharing insights. Their energy tends to be expressive, up beat and casual. They tend to take ideas and create new approaches that are helpful.

General Observations	
ESTP	ENTP
ESTPs show an interest in practical reality and "doing," more than studying. Their **concise, colourful language** will tend to get to the point quickly. In debate, they may change their view if presented with countering data. **ESTPs** use **Contextual Thinking**: relating everything to the present context. ESTPs tend to build **fraternal relationships**: when they are working in a team there will be a sense of everyone being "buddies." When the context is changed, the relationship may not continue, because there is a new context to explore.	**ENTPs** enjoy exploring hypotheses for the sake of intellectual rigor. Their **precise, accurate language** shows when they correct the word choice of others. In debate, they may have difficulty accepting data that is contrary to their mental model. **ENTPs** use **Differential Thinking**: searching for distinctions and differences in models, facts and theories. ENTPs tend to build **expert relationships**: if a person has a source of knowledge or expertise, whatever their role, then that builds credibility and the relationship tends to last while that remains an expertise of interest.

QUESTIONS FOR SORTING BETWEEN IMPROVISER AND THEORIST TEMPERAMENTS

What drives you? What do you really enjoy doing?

Listen for the **Improviser's (ESTP)** drive for freedom, seeing results in the moment, making an impact, and being noticed.

Listen for the **Theorist's (ENTP)** drive for competence, intellectual rigor, and strategic focus.

What do you really struggle with? When was a time you felt you have failed?

- Listen for **Improvisers (ESTP)** to describe long-term projects, with no tangible outcome, too many rules, and pointless details. ESTPs may also describe failure as being unacknowledged.
- Listen for **Theorists (ENTP)** to describe failure as perceiving themselves to have said or done something that was stupid or to have obviously failed. ENTPs may also struggle with the implementation of ideas (an area where ESTPs excel).

QUESTIONS TO IDENTIFY EXPERIENCING (SE) VERSUS BRAINSTORMING (NE)

Are you tuned in to physical changes of body language? Do you get easily distracted by your environment?

- If **Yes**, consider **Improviser (ESTP)** because Improvisers using **Experiencing (Se)** tend to pick up changes in the external environment and may be distracted by physical concrete data.

- If **No**, consider **Theorist (ENTP)** because Theorists using **Brainstorming (Ne)** tend to focus more on ideas and concepts. Therefore they are not as aware of the concrete realities of the external environment.

QUESTIONS TO CLARIFY TEMPERAMENT VIA CURRENT IMPACT OR FUTURE DIRECTION

Do you need to see immediate concrete results from your efforts?

- If **Yes**, consider **ESTP** because **Improvisers** tend to drive toward tangible results. Instant gratification takes too long!
- If **No**, consider **ENTP** because **Theorists** don't necessarily need a tangible result from their work, if they feel they have gained knowledge, expertise or learning from the endeavour.

Do you tend to focus on the here and now? Do you trust the future to take care of itself?

- If **Yes**, consider **Improviser (ESTP)** because Improvisers tend to live in the present and seize the moment.
- If **No**, consider **Theorist (ENTP)** as Theorists tend to be future-focused with a strategy to achieve their ultimate goal.

QUESTIONS TO CLARIFY INTERACTION STYLE

Are you comfortable telling people what to do?

- If **Yes**, consider **ESTP** because **In Charge Improvisers** have a preference for **Directing** communication and tend to be explicit in giving instructions about who is going to do what by when.
- If **No**, consider **ENTP** because **Get Things Going Theorists** have a preference for **Informing** communication and tend to make statements or give information and allow the other person to decide what they are going to do.

Are you stressed when it appears that nothing is happening?

- If **Yes**, consider **ESTP** because **In Charge Improvisers** like to know that action is being taken towards the goal.
- If **No**, consider **ENTP** because **Get Things Going Theorists** are comfortable with the emergent process when exploring possibilities.

6. Distinguishing ESTP from ENTP: Review

EXERCISE 21: DISTINGUISHING BETWEEN ESTP AND ENTP

Thinking of these two personality types:

- Which temperament seems like the best fit and why? Improviser (ESTP) or Theorist (ENTP)?
- Which information gathering function-attitude appears to be the best fit and why? Experiencing (Se) or Brainstorming (Ne)?
- Which Interaction Style seems like the best fit and why? In Charge or Get Things Going?
- What developmental factors might be relevant in selecting best-fit type?

TRY IT ON!

DISTINGUISHING BETWEEN ESTP AND ENTP

Which temperament seems like the best fit and why? Improviser (ESTP) or Theorist (ENTP)?

_____

_____

Which information gathering function-attitude appears to be the best fit and why? Experiencing (Se) or Brainstorming (Ne)?

_____

_____

Which Interaction Style seems like the best fit and why? In Charge or Get Things Going?

_____

_____

What developmental factors might be relevant in selecting best-fit type?

_____

_____

7. DISTINGUISHING ENTP FROM ENFP

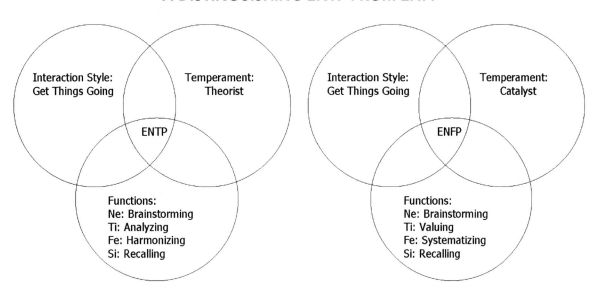

There are several **core similarities** between **ENFPs** and **ENTPs**. For both types, energy flows out to the external world first (**Extraverting** Preference) which means that they tend to be enthusiastic, verbally fluent and quick thinking. Both share an **iNtuiting** preference and therefore tend to use abstract language as they talk about concepts, theories and models. Both share **Brainstorming (Ne)** as their Adult function and they therefore tend to live in the world of possibilities, reading between the lines and being attune to subtle patterns and meanings in the external world. Those who have Brainstorming in this Adult position appear naturally optimistic and positive. In addition, both types share the **Get Things Going** Interaction Style. Individuals who use his style when trying to influence others like to initiate interactions, motivate others to be involved and facilitate discussion and engagement. Their energy tends to be expressive, casual and up beat. They both tend to make consensual decisions and can be stressed by not being involved. In addition, as both share the **Perceiving** preference, they tend to be flexible, open-ended and comfortable with adapting to new situations. Finally as they both share Balancing **Recalling (Si)**, as they mature you may see them using this function in a positive way to put a reality check on hypotheses.

There are also **marked differences** between **ENTPs** and **ENFPs**.

ENTP	ENFP
Temperament	
ENTPs have a **Theorist** temperament. Theorists need to have access to knowledge, be competent, and have control over their own destiny. Theorists tend to be future-focused and are driven to see things from a strategic, long-term perspective. Theorists excel at presenting a logical point of view and value intellectual independence	**ENFPs** have a **Catalyst** temperament. Catalysts need to have a purpose and meaning, be special, and have authentic one-on-one relationships. Catalysts tend to be passionate about helping people develop their potential and are on a quest for unique identity. Catalysts tend to work well with individuals as they use empathy to put themselves in other people's shoes.
Stress Response Each stress response can cause the temperament to act diametrically differently from their innate abilities.	
Theorists (ENTP) may appear very aloof, emotionally cut off, impersonal, and look excessively failure avoidant when they perceive themselves to have failed. The paradox of this stress response is to move from competent to incompetent.	**Catalysts (ENFP)** may hide his or her true self with a pretend problem or false identity or sacrifice their wants and needs to please others when they perceive themselves to be not unique. The paradox of this stress response is to move from genuine to phony.

ENTP	ENFP
Decision Making Function-attitudes	
ENTPs use **Analyzing (Ti)** which involves making decisions by gathering logical data and evaluating it against internal criteria. Those who use Analyzing (Ti) with ease excel at dissecting an argument, creating a unique point of view, and approaching problems from various reasonable perspectives. As they mature, they are able to access their Child **Harmonizing (Fe)** function which can manifest itself as the social organizer. This can sometimes look like the person has a Feeling preference.	**ENFPs** use **Valuing (Fi)** which involves making decisions by evaluating data against an internal beliefs system. Those who use Valuing (Fi) with ease tend to be private in sharing their innermost thoughts, tolerant of individual differences, and driven to achieve alignment between their internal values and the external world. As they mature, they are able to access their Child **Systematizing (Te)** function which can manifest as organizing social events. This can sometimes look like the person has a Thinking preference.

General Observations	
ENTPs enjoy exploring hypotheses for the sake of intellectual rigor. Their **precise, accurate language** shows when they correct the word choice of others. In debate, they may have difficulty accepting data that is contrary to their mental model, and will use critical questioning to clarify ideas and evaluate the feasibility of other possibilities.	**ENFPs** enjoy learning about the theory of human behaviours, particularly in helping people get more out of life. Their **global, metaphorical language** will often include generalizations, and they will talk about impressions versus specific data. Their more flowing communication style may appear to "meander" and include non-sequitors.

General Observations	
ENTPs are one of the **pragmatic** temperaments (as with Improvisers) which means that they tend to act in accordance with what they see needs to be done. They therefore tend to focus more on independence and seek the action that will achieve the goal in the most effective way.	**ENFPs** are one of the collaborative temperaments (as with Stabilizers) which means that they tend to act in community with a sense of what is good for the people. Therefore they tend to focus more on interdependence and seek cooperative action that achieve the goals with agreement from the group.
ENTPs tend to demonstrate the **strategic skill** set using their intuitive, logical talents to constantly explore multiple possibilities and discern the link between ends and means.	**ENFPs** tend to demonstrate the **diplomatic skill** set using their intuitive, values-based talents to constantly explore multiple possibilities to build bridges and connect apparently disparate points of view.

QUESTIONS FOR SORTING BETWEEN THEORIST AND CATALYST TEMPERAMENTS

What drives you? What do you really enjoy doing?
- Listen for the **Theorist's (ENTP)** need for competence, intellectual independence, and strategic focus.
- Listen **for Catalyst's (ENFP)** need for significant relationships and drive to develop people and their potential.

What do you really struggle with? When was a time that you felt you had not succeeded?
- Listen for **Theorists (ENTP)** to describe failure as perceiving themselves to have said or done something that was stupid or to have obviously failed. ENTPs may also struggle with feeling out of control and having no challenge or independence.

- Listen for **Catalysts (ENFP)** to describe failure as being betrayed, being made to feel undervalued or receiving no positive feedback. ENFPs may also struggle when receiving only developmental feedback and having too many details to manage.

Do you always see the impact on people when making decisions?
- If **Yes,** consider **ENFP** because **Catalysts** naturally tend to consider the emotional issues, and want decisions to be fair to those involved.
- If **No** consider **ENTP** because **Theorists** tend to focus on the logical principles first and approach decisions more pragmatically.

Are you aware of how people are responding to you?
- If **Yes** consider **Catalyst (ENFP)** because Catalysts using empathy are very aware of individual responses and feelings around a different point of view.
- If **No** consider **Theorist (ENTP)** because Theorists may tend to be oblivious of interpersonal dynamics as they focus on the logical arguments to support their point of view.

QUESTIONS FOR DISTINGUISHING BETWEEN ANALYZING (TI) AND VALUING (FI)

Has there been a time when someone crossed your values and you broke off that relationship?
- If **Yes,** consider **Catalyst (ENFP)** using **Valuing (Fi)** because if something happens that crossed their core beliefs, they will often completely disconnect from that relationship or organization.
- If **No,** consider **Theorist (ENTP)** using **Analyzing (Ti)** because the logic and the desire for social harmony may take precedence.

Do you naturally tend to use critical questioning to clarify a point of view?
- If **Yes,** consider **Theorist (ENTP)** using **Analyzing (Ti)** because critical questioning is a tool that is used to check for inconsistencies and ascertain the resilience of an argument.
- If **No,** consider **Catalyst (ENFP)** using **Valuing (Fi)** because the natural tendency of Valuing is to respect and tolerate many different points of view (as long as none of these appear in opposition to their values.)

7. Distinguishing ENTP from ENFP: Review

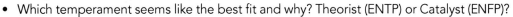

EXERCISE 22: DISTINGUISHING BETWEEN ENTP AND ENFP

Thinking of these two personality types:

- Which temperament seems like the best fit and why? Theorist (ENTP) or Catalyst (ENFP)?
- Which decision making function-attitude appears to be the best fit and why? Analyzing (Ti) or Valuing (Fi)?
- What other developmental factors might be relevant in selecting best-fit type and how?

TRY IT ON!

DISTINGUISHING BETWEEN ENTP AND ENFP

Which temperament seems like the best fit and why? Theorist (ENTP) or Catalyst (ENFP)?

_____

_____

Which decision making function-attitude appears to be the best fit and why? Analyzing (Ti) or Valuing (Fi)?

_____

_____

What other developmental factors might be relevant in selecting best-fit type and how?

_____

_____

8. DISTINGUISHING ESFP FROM ENFP

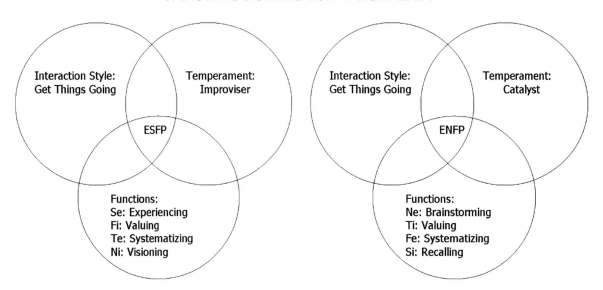

ESFPs a and **ENFPs** share certain **core similarities.** Both types can look similar because they both tend to be high energy, fun, people-focused, and spontaneous. Both share an **Extraverting** preference and so their energy gravitates out first to the external world of people and events. As a result they may demonstrate more expressive body language, tend to talk everything over and respond with enthusiasm. ESFPs and ENFPs share the **Get Things Going** Interaction Style which means that they both believe that it is worth the time it takes to involve others in order to achieve an embraced decision. They may both feel stressed if they are not included or feel unliked, and as a result may become scattered or overly expressive. Both types are tuned into the external world to gather data and see options and opportunities. With that information, they make decisions using the same Parent function-attitude: **Valuing (Fi).** Valuing involves making a subjective decision using an internal beliefs system. Those who use Valuing with ease (Fi) tend to be tolerant of individual differences, private in sharing their innermost thoughts, and driven to live in alignment with their own internal values. They both share the **Perceiving** preference which means that they view time as more elastic and may tend to leave options open so as not to restrict their choice.

However, despite these similarities there are also a number of **marked differences ESFPs** and **ENFPs.** The following table highlights a few of these key indicators.

ESFP	ENFP
Temperament	
ESFPs have an **Improviser** temperament. Improvisers need a sense of freedom, the ability to act in the moment and enjoy the here and now. Improvisers tend to make the most of any situation and are talented at seizing current opportunities. Improvisers tend to work well with individuals because they innately recognize the motive of the other person: what they want out of a specific situation.	**ENFPs** have a **Catalyst** temperament. Catalysts need a sense of purpose and meaning, the ability to be special, and tend to be future-focused. Catalysts tend to be passionate about helping people develop their potential and are talented at building bridges between disparate points of view. Catalysts tend to work well with individuals because they use empathy to put themselves in other people's shoes: what meaning or purpose is important to them.
Stress Response Each stress response can cause the temperament to act diametrically differently from their innate abilities.	
Improvisers (ESFPs) may leave projects to the last minute or not deliver on projects to cause a reaction. The paradox of this stress response is to move from impressive to unimpressive.	Catalysts (ENFPs) may project negative attributions to others and vent without checking out what's really going on in a negative situation. The paradox of this stress response is to move from empathetic to unfeeling.

ESFP	ENFP
Function-Attitudes	
ESFPs use **Experiencing (Se)**. They read all the concrete data in the moment – sound, sight, smell, taste, and touch. Using Experiencing **(Se)** in this way, will often mean they will pick up minute changes in facial expression, movements in body language, and comment on them. Using Experiencing (Se) may also mean that they only see the here and now and may miss the hidden implications in a situation.	**ENFPs** use **Brainstorming (Ne)**. They tend to read between the lines and infer meaning from data. Using Brainstorming (Ne) in this way, will often mean that they will make conclusions or read meaning about people or situations, but may not be able to give the specific source of the impressions. Using Brainstorming (Ne) may also mean that they are so absorbed in ideas that they are oblivious to current sensory data.

General Observations	
ESFPs tend to show an interest in practical reality and having fun with people, versus hypothesizing about behaviours. Their **concise, colourful** language will tend to get to the point quickly and will often be used to amuse colleagues and friends. Their literal communication style tends to "cut through" unnecessary detail.	**ENFPs** enjoy learning about the theory of human behaviours, particularly in helping people get more out of life. Their **global language** will often include generalizations, metaphors and talk about impressions versus specifics. Their more flowing style may appear to "meander" and include non-sequitors.
ESFPs tend to use **Contextual Thinking**; the ability to see how things fit and notice when things are not as they should be. This enables them to seize current opportunities.	**ESFPs** tend to use **Integrative Thinking**; the ability to see and link similarities between multiple subjects and/or theories. This enables them to create meaning from disparate ideas.
ESFPs are one of the **Pragmatic** temperaments (with Theorists) which means that they tend to value independence and enjoy roles where they are able to take action to do what works.	**ENFPs** are one of the **Collaborative** temperaments (with Stabilizers) which means that they tend to value interdependence and enjoy roles where they are able to help people utilize their unique talents.
ESFPs tend to build **fraternal relationships**: everyone is on the same level and are "buddies."	**ENFPs** tend to build **empathic relationships** where each is a genuine, intense, one-on-one connection.

QUESTIONS FOR SORTING BETWEEN IMPROVISER AND CATALYST TEMPERAMENTS

What drives you? What do you really enjoy doing?

- Listen for **Improviser's (ESFP)** drive for freedom, fun and seeing results in the moment, making an impact and being noticed.
- Listen for **Catalyst's (ENFP)** drive for purpose, meaning and significance and to be seen as special.

What do you really struggle with? When was a time that you felt you had failed?

- Listen for **Improvisers (ESFP)** to describe long-term projects, with no tangible outcome, too many rules, and pointless details.
- Listen for **Catalysts (ENFP)** to describe failure as being betrayed, being made to feel undervalued or receiving no positive feedback, or lots of developmental feedback.

QUESTIONS TO CLARIFY TEMPERAMENT VIA CURRENT IMPACT OR FUTURE DIRECTION

Do you need to see immediate concrete results from your efforts?

- If **Yes,** consider **ESFP** because **Improvisers** tend to drive toward tangible results. Instant gratification is not soon enough!
- If **No,** consider **ENFP** because **Catalysts** don't necessarily need to see a concrete outcome if they feel they have "touched" individuals and helped them get more out of their lives.

Do you tend to focus on the here and now? Do you trust the future to take care of itself?

- If **Yes** consider **Improviser (ESFP)** because **Improvisers** live in the present and seize the moment.
- If **No,** consider **Catalyst (ENFP)** because **Catalysts** tend to be future-focused on their journey in support of their cause.

QUESTIONS TO IDENTIFY EXPERIENCING (SE) VERSUS BRAINSTORMING (NE)

Are you tuned in to physical changes of body language? Are you easily distracted by your environment?

- If **Yes,** consider **Improviser (ESFP)** because Improvisers using **Experiencing (Se)** tend to pick up changes in the external environment and may be distracted by physical concrete data.
- If **No,** consider **Catalyst (ENFP)** because Catalysts using **Brainstorming (Ne)** may tend to be more oblivious to physical clues as they focus on people's individuality and potential.

Do you tend to gravitate towards ideas if they have immediate practical application?

- If **Yes,** consider **Improviser (ESFP)** because Improvisers using **Experiencing (Se)** enjoy looking at options which they can act upon.
- If **No,** consider **Catalyst (ENFP)** because Catalysts using **Brainstorming (Ne)** enjoy exploring ideas, possibilities and hypotheses without any necessary immediate application.

8. Distinguishing ESFP from ENFP: Review

EXERCISE 23: DISTINGUISHING BETWEEN ESFP AND ENFP

Thinking of these two personality types:

- Which temperament seems like the best fit and why? Improviser (ESFP) or Catalyst (ENFP)?
- Which information gathering function-attitude appears to be the best fit and why? Experiencing (Se) or Brainstorming (Ne)?
- What other developmental factors might be relevant in selecting best-fit type and how?

TRY IT ON!

DISTINGUISHING BETWEEN ESFP AND ENFP

Which temperament seems like the best fit and why? Improviser (ESFP) or Catalyst (ENFP)?

_____

_____

Which information gathering function-attitude appears to be the best fit and why? Experiencing (Se) or Brainstorming (Ne)?

_____

_____

What other developmental factors might be relevant in selecting best-fit type and how?

_____

_____

SUMMARY

As you can see, when individuals with the Extraverting preference share three "letters" out of four, it can be tempting to see these types as similar. However it is possible to have an in-depth exploration to ensure that best-fit type has been identified by exploring the personality further using the lenses of:

- Temperament
- Information Gathering Function-Attitudes
- Decision Making Function-Attitudes
- Hierarchy of Function-Attitudes
- Interaction Style

SCORECARD
- What did you learn from comparing similar type pairs?
- How will this approach help you in clarifying best-fit type?
- How else can you build your knowledge of the multiple lenses of type?

Type Descriptions

IMPROVISERS

TYPE	ESTP: EXTRAVERTED TACTICIAN
DESCRIPTION	**Extraverted Tacticians** are high-energy, action-oriented, quick-thinking, objective decision-makers. Their focus on making things happen can make them appear impatient with slow-moving, theoretical discussion and concepts. They are direct and their word choice focuses on "netting it out" or getting to the point. They possess intense observation skills, can tune in to what's happening in the moment, are acutely aware of non-verbal cues and then respond as needed. Their minds move so rapidly that often their words are left behind, as they push on for a result or to make an impact. They constantly find new ways of doing things. Sometimes perceived as uncaring by their team members, they nonetheless protect the people who are important to them.
TEMPERAMENT	Improviser Need to act in the moment, be impressive and produce immediate concrete tangible results.

INTERACTION STYLE	**In Charge** Like to move quickly towards a goal. Manoeuvring rapidly to take action in the now moment. Tend to appear quick moving, confident and determined.
DIRECTION OF ENERGY	Extraverting Energy goes outwards: process externally and tend to initiate interaction.
FIRST FUNCTION (ADULT)	Experiencing (Se) Rapid uptake of sensory data in the now moment from the external world. Acute awareness of specifics and realities in the world around them.
SECOND FUNCTION (PARENT)	Analyzing (Ti) Make decisions using internal logical criteria and principles. Analyze how and why things work.
THIRD FUNCTION (CHILD)	Harmonizing (Fe) Will be aware of subjective criteria to optimize group interaction. May appear gregarious and empathetic.
SHADOW FUNCTION (BALANCING)	Visioning (Ni) Will occasionally gather information by creating their own complete idea or future direction. Will verify with sensory data. When under stress their perception might be negatively distorted to perceive doom and gloom.
STRENGTHS ON A TEAM	Optimistic can-do attitude. Excellent negotiators: play to win. Realistic, hands-on, logical problem solvers. Action oriented implementers.
POTENTIAL CHALLENGES ON A TEAM	May get bored easily if concrete tangible progress is not made. May work around rules and not get to the root cause of a problem. May appear autonomous "calling their own shots."
AS A LEADER	Are able to think on their feet. Focus is on action. Quickly able to recognize opportunities and get things moving. Rolls up his/her sleeves and gets involved.
WORKS BEST WITH	Lots of freedom and fun. As few rules as possible and the ability to take risks.
WORKS LEAST WELL WITH	Lots of moaning. Individuals who talk things through without any apparent action.

TYPE	ISTP: INTROVERTED TACTICIAN
DESCRIPTION	**Introverted Tacticians** live in the present and act in the moment to get to the root cause, and solve problems. They are the most analytical of the Improvisers, enjoying theoretical constructs with practical reasoning. They can absorb large amounts of impersonal facts and have a high affiliation with numbers. They thrive on variety and focus on doing what needs to be done with the least amount of fuss. They will change direction readily as additional information becomes available and maneuver systems to meet their ends. They are adept with tools and are able to reason impersonally and objectively. They may alienate their teammates with their apparent manipulation, but then working in teams is a game to them.
TEMPERAMENT	Improviser Need to act in the moment, be impressive, and produce immediate concrete tangible results.
INTERACTION STYLE	**Chart the Course** Like to think ahead and predict the goal. Evaluating the most logical plan of attack based on the current reality. Tend to appear calm, intense and focused.
DIRECTION OF ENERGY	Introverting Energy goes inwards: tend to process and reflect and respond to personal interaction.
FIRST FUNCTION (ADULT)	Analyzing (Ti) Make decisions using their internal logical criteria and principles. Analyze how and why things work. Always approaching data from an independent perspective, with their own logical point of view.
SECOND FUNCTION (PARENT)	Experiencing (Se) Rapid uptake of sensory data in the now moment from the external world. Acute awareness of specifics and realities in the world around them.
THIRD FUNCTION (CHILD)	Visioning (Ni) Will occasionally gather information by creating their own complete idea, particularly when solving problems. Will verify with sensory data.
SHADOW FUNCTION (BALANCING)	Harmonizing (Fe) Will be aware of subjective criteria to optimize group interaction. When under stress may show emotional reactions such as anger and frustration with sharp outbursts. May be uncomfortable with displays of emotion from others.

STRENGTHS ON A TEAM	Confident, independent and determined. Believe in economy of effort. Concretely analytical – can dissect arguments. Naturally adept with tools and numbers.
POTENTIAL CHALLENGES ON A TEAM	May appear overly critical and cynical when questioning to clarify logic. May lack long-term vision and an understanding of how their behaviour affects others. May appear indifferent to others needs.
AS A LEADER	Great tactical trouble shooter. Expects a tolerance for ambiguity from team. Willing to gamble for big stakes.
WORKS BEST WITH	Working solo with the ability to fight fires at will. A variety of short-term projects.
WORKS LEAST WELL WITH	Team members who display intense emotional reactions. Individuals who are very demanding.

TYPE	ESFP: EXTRAVERTED PERFORMER
DESCRIPTION	**Extraverted Improvisers** are colourful, free-spirited, and people-focused. Using their acute sensory inputs they make decisions based on what is in alignment with their internal values system. They are interested in people and new experiences, as they live in the moment. They are generous of spirit, active, talkative and flexible. Their natural exuberance attracts others as they get the task done with the maximum amount of fun and minimum amount of fuss. They find enjoyment in food, clothes, animals, the natural world, and activities. They work best in a flexible, unstructured environment. Their tendency to perform in groups and see the light-hearted side may make other team members want them to be more serious.
TEMPERAMENT	Improviser Need to act in the moment, be impressive, produce immediate concrete tangible results.
INTERACTION STYLE	Get Things Going Like to facilitate involvement from the group. Using playfulness to help others feel valued and involved. Tend to appear expressive, up beat and casual.

DIRECTION OF ENERGY	Extraverting Energy goes outwards: process externally and tend to initiate interaction.
FIRST FUNCTION (ADULT)	Experiencing (Se) Rapid uptake of sensory data in the now moment from the external world. Acute awareness of specifics and realities in the world around them. Able to read sensory data in the moment.
SECOND FUNCTION (PARENT)	Valuing (Fi) Make decisions quietly, but firmly based on their own internal beliefs system. Guided by strong inner values and wish life to be in congruence with those beliefs. Tolerant of differences and adaptable until the values system is crossed then can appear rigid.
THIRD FUNCTION (CHILD)	Systematizing (Te) Will make some decisions using logical criteria to plan and organize logistics and events in the external world.
SHADOW FUNCTION (BALANCING)	Visioning (Ni) Will occasionally gather information by creating their own complete idea or future direction. Ideas may "pop" into their minds. Will verify with sensory data. When under stress my get stuck in here and now with an inability to step back for the "aha."
STRENGTHS ON A TEAM	Optimistic can-do attitude. Friendly, energetic generous and people focused. Practical problem solving – pick up possible issues quickly. Able to interact easily with different team members.
POTENTIAL CHALLENGES ON A TEAM	May get bored easily if work appears to be impractical. May appear to be too playful and not serious about work. May try to juggle too many projects.
AS A LEADER	Informal, social and easy going with a focus on concrete results. Seeks quick results and fosters collaboration. Excellent at stimulating the team to perform and encouraging team mates.
WORKS BEST WITH	Freedom and challenge. Opportunity to solve problems in the moment.
WORKS LEAST WELL WITH/WHEN	When there is too much structure and processes. Working on long-term abstract issues.

TYPE	ISFP: INTROVERTED PERFORMER
DESCRIPTION	**Introverted Improvisers** live in the present and prize the freedom to follow their own course. They are faithful at fulfilling obligations to people and things that are important to them. They often appear as unassuming, easy-going, gentle, and soft-spoken. They will provide help in concrete tangible ways, and with their observation skills, have a gift of expressing abstract things concretely. Their playful sense of humour may not be seen until they are comfortable with you. They will adapt well to new situations and approach life from a "Don't worry be happy" perspective. In teams, their tendency to be laid back in their approach could be viewed as lack of interest or direction.
TEMPERAMENT	Improviser Need to act in the moment, be impressive, and produce immediate concrete tangible results.
INTERACTION STYLE	Behind the Scenes Like to take the time to reconcile many inputs. Supporting those that they care about through their actions. Tend to appear approachable, friendly and patient.
DIRECTION OF ENERGY	Introverting Energy goes inwards: tend to process and reflect, don't see all emotions.
FIRST FUNCTION (ADULT)	Valuing (Fi) Makes decisions quietly, but firmly based on their own internal beliefs system. Guided by strong inner values and wish life to be in congruence with those beliefs. Tolerant of individual differences and easy going until those values are challenged.
SECOND FUNCTION (PARENT)	Experiencing (Se) Rapid uptake of sensory data in the now moment from the external world. Acute awareness of specifics and realities in the world around them.
THIRD FUNCTION (CHILD)	Visioning (Ni) Will occasionally gather information by creating their own complete idea or future direction. Will verify with sensory data. Ideas will suddenly appear.
SHADOW FUNCTION (BALANCING)	Systematizing (Te) Will make some decisions using logical criteria to plan and organize logistics and events in the external world. When under stress, they may obsess about details and creating organization.

STRENGTHS ON A TEAM	Contributes deep loyalty to the team. Easy going but with the ability to provide sensible solutions to practical problems. Quiet sense of fun. Humane with the ability to persuade others in a non-confrontational way.
POTENTIAL CHALLENGES ON A TEAM	May not speak up about what he or she wants. May appear indecisive as criteria are internally evaluated against what is fair May withdraw from anger and tension and not address the core issue.
AS A LEADER	Creates supportive egalitarian atmosphere. Sets realistic achievable goals. Lead by doing rather than telling and adapt quickly to external changes.
WORKS BEST WITH	Close informal relationships in a physically pleasant environment. Flexible environment with few rules.
WORKS LEAST WELL WITH/WHEN	Interpersonal conflict. Having to plan and organize activities within a fixed deadline.

STABILIZERS

TYPE	ESTJ: EXTRAVERTED ORGANIZER
DESCRIPTION	**Extraverted Organizers** are detail-oriented, high-energy decision-makers. They drive for closure with the aim of organizing, planning and structuring the external environment. The most "driven" of the Stabilizers, they take action to get things done, in a systematic and consistent way. They take an objective approach to problem solving and can be tough when the situation demands. They enjoy activity that produces concrete tangible results and are adept at creating systems that assign responsibilities and allocate resources. They enjoy interacting with others, especially around games and team activities. As team members they set high standards and have a clear sense of "right and wrong."
TEMPERAMENT	Stabilizer Need to be part of a group/team, fulfil responsibilities, make a contribution therein.
INTERACTION STYLE	**In Charge** Like to move quickly towards a goal. Making rapid decisions to organize and structure current reality. Tend to appear quick moving, confident and determined.
DIRECTION OF ENERGY	**Extraverting** Energy goes outwards: process externally and tend to initiate interaction.
FIRST FUNCTION (ADULT)	Systematizing (Te) Making decisions to achieve goals using logical criteria to plan and organize logistics and events in the external world. Adept at sequencing tasks and resources to achieve an end goal. Strong push for closure. Very action oriented.
SECOND FUNCTION (PARENT)	Recalling (Si) Gather information by referring back to a rich databank of past sensory experiences which are compared and contrasted to the present. Able to bring the best of the past into the future. Monitors and evaluates for reality.
THIRD FUNCTION (CHILD)	Brainstorming (Ne) Some external exploration of future possibilities, patterns, and meaning building on concrete experienced information.

SHADOW FUNCTION (BALANCING)	Valuing (Fi) May consider their internal values and beliefs, but this decision will be subservient to logical criteria. When under stress, this function appears as a rigid adherence to "right and wrong."
STRENGTHS ON A TEAM	Contributes hard work to complete activities. Economical with resources. Ability to set up and implement systems. Sees the right way to get the job done and focus on timely completion.
POTENTIAL CHALLENGES ON A TEAM	May dismiss ideas which they perceive to be impractical. May appear too driven for closure and uncomfortable with ambiguity. May appear to ignore team members' feelings in their push to complete the work.
AS A LEADER	Confident down-to-earth approach. Sets clear measurable targets with implementation plans. Respects systems and procedures for monitoring of performance.
WORKS BEST WITH	An environment where they can make things happen. A structured role working with experienced team members.
WORKS LEAST WELL WITH/WHEN	Team members are sloppy and "break the rules." There is constant change and no access to reliable data.

TYPE	ISTJ: INTROVERTED ORGANIZERS
DESCRIPTION	**Introverted Organizers** are logical, practical, organized, and thorough. They rely on historic experience from which to create concrete action plans. They will create processes and procedures to smooth workflow, eliminate redundancy and achieve economy of effort. They are loyal and dutiful, and work with steady energy to ensure commitments are met on time. They tend to prefer to have time alone and may appear serious and orderly. They trust facts, are task-oriented and can manage extensive detail. They work hard at whatever they do, and, once a skill is learned, they perform it with competence. As team members they are dedicated and committed but may frustrate their colleagues in their sequential, one thing at a time, approach combined with a reluctance to change.

TEMPERAMENT	Stabilizer Need to be part of a group or a team, fulfil responsibilities, and make a contribution therein.
INTERACTION STYLE	Chart the Course Like to think ahead and predict the goal. Reviewing previous experience to think through the most systematic plan. Tend to appear calm, intense and focused.
DIRECTION OF ENERGY	Introverting Energy goes inwards: tend to process and reflect, don't see all emotions.
FIRST FUNCTION (ADULT)	Recalling (Si) Gather information by referring to a rich databank of past sensory experiences and comparing and contrasting these to the present. Able to bring the best of the past to the future and audit the reality of any given situation.
SECOND FUNCTION (PARENT)	Systematizing (Te) Making decisions using logical criteria to plan and organize logistics and events in the external world. Sequence events and resources to achieve goals in a timely manner.
SHADOW FUNCTION (CHILD)	Valuing (Fi) May consider their internal values and beliefs, but this decision will be subservient to logical criteria.
SHADOW FUNCTION (BALANCING)	Brainstorming (Ne) Some external exploration of future possibilities, patterns and meaning building on previously experienced events. When under stress this function-attitude may imply distorted patterns and meanings and foresee doom and gloom.
STRENGTHS ON A TEAM	Quiet dedicated and organized: great follow through skills. Thorough, dependable and trustworthy. No nonsense, hard-working team members who deliver on responsibilities given clearly defined roles. Meticulous attendion to detail and aims for perfection.
POTENTIAL CHALLENGES ON A TEAM	May appear rigid about time schedules and rules: go by the book. Instead of delegating my get bogged down in details. May neglect the big picture and people when focused on task completion.

AS A LEADER	Thorough and thoughtful planning of team activity. Sets clear targets and defines clear accountabilities. Guards against waste and can make tough decisions.
WORKS BEST WITH	Hard working, organized people who understand the importance of completing projects on time. Periods of alone time to focus on their own deliverables.
WORKS LEAST WELL WITH	Dynamic, unstructured environments with no clearly defined or constantly changing goals. Teams who seem to crave lots of personal interaction and what could be perceived as "touchy-feely" activities.

TYPE	ESFJ: EXTRAVERTED PROTECTOR
DESCRIPTION	**Extraverted Protectors** are warm, personable, and outgoing. They enjoy harmonious team environments, working within that structure to ensure that organization is established and responsibilities are met. They are conscientious and loyal, and value security and stability. They use information from their extensive databank of past sensory experiences to apply in their concrete, task-focused work. They are energized by being with others and are genuinely interested in others lives and concerns. They enjoy participating in committees and are good at organizing celebrations and preserving traditions. As team members, they will gravitate to being the organizer of all team and individual celebrations, yet may sometimes overload themselves with responsibilities.
TEMPERAMENT	Stabilizer Need to be part of a group or a team, fulfil responsibilities, and make a contribution therein.
INTERACTION STYLE	Get Things Going Like to facilitate involvement from the group. Organizing tasks to make life harmonious and easier. Tend to appear expressive, up beat and casual
DIRECTION OF ENERGY	Extraverting Energy goes outwards: process externally and tend to initiate interaction.
FIRST FUNCTION (ADULT)	Harmonizing (Fe) Making decisions using subjective criteria to optimize group harmony. Sensitive to other people's wants and needs. Self discloses to connect, but may show emotions on face when stressed.

SECOND FUNCTION (PARENT)	Recalling (Si) Gather information by referring to a rich databank of past sensory experiences and comparing and contrasting these to the present. Able to audit events and data for reality.
SHADOW FUNCTION (CHILD)	Brainstorming (Ne) Some external exploration of future possibilities, patterns and meaning building on concrete experienced information.
SHADOW FUNCTION (BALANCING)	Analyzing (Ti) May compare and contrast data against an internal model, but this will be superseded by appropriateness to the group. When in stress, this function can appear as overly critical, questioning logic and rationale.
STRENGTHS ON A TEAM	Energetic, enthusiastic and warm. Like helping others who want to do likewise. Aware of and cater to others needs. Responsible and focus on building team cohesiveness.
POTENTIAL CHALLENGES ON A TEAM	May avoid conflict. May make decisions based on individuals' needs and appear illogical at times. May seem too talkative as they involve others in the team activities.
AS A LEADER	Likes to discuss his/her way to achieve consensus. Gives and expects personal loyalty and hard work. Ready with positive feedback for good work and advice if team members have issues they are facing.
WORKS BEST WITH	A culture which is organized and somewhat predictable. A structure where their people skills can contribute to tangible results.
WORKS LEAST WELL WHEN	There is a lot of conflict and back biting. There is a lot of criticism.

TYPE	ISFJ: INTROVERTED PROTECTOR
DESCRIPTION	**Introverted Protectors** are stable, supportive, empathetic team members who work tirelessly behind the scenes to achieve team goals. They are concrete, task-focused, and value possessions and economy of resources. Valuing traditions and historic experience, they make decisions that will meet the needs of the group. When communicating, they follow a detailed, sequential, step-by-step thought process and tend to establish orderly procedures. They enjoy helping others, are dependable and considerate, and gravitate to roles that involve service to others. Maintaining the cohesiveness of the team and living up to their responsibilities are fundamental to the way they operate. As team members, they have to be careful that they are not taken advantage of, because they will do tasks for others in such an unassuming way, the effort goes unnoticed.
TEMPERAMENT	Stabilizer Need to be part of a group or a team, fulfil responsibilities, and make a contribution therein.
INTERACTION STYLE	Behind the Scenes Like to take the time to reconcile many inputs. Integrating previous experience to support the team in the safest way. Tend to appear approachable, friendly and patient.
DIRECTION OF ENERGY	Introverting Energy goes inwards: tend to process and reflect, don't see all emotions.
FIRST FUNCTION (ADULT)	Recalling (Si) Gather information by referring to a rich databank of past sensory experiences and comparing and contrasting these to the present. Able to bring to the current task an accurate assessment of what is real.
SECOND FUNCTION (PARENT)	Harmonizing (Fe) Making decisions using subjective criteria to optimize group harmony. Sensitive to and considerate of other people's feelings.
SHADOW FUNCTION (CHILD)	Analyzing (Ti) May compare and contrast data against an internal model, but this will be superseded by appropriateness to the group.
SHADOW FUNCTION (BALANCING)	Brainstorming (Ne) Some external exploration of future possibilities, patterns and meaning building on past sensory experience. When under stress, this function may negative fantasize and perceive "doom and gloom."

STRENGTHS ON A TEAM	Conscientious: will probably pick up tasks which others may have dropped. Work with steady energy to plan and follow through team activities. Look after others on the team with an established structure. Strong tactical implementers who use contingency planning.
POTENTIAL CHALLENGES ON A TEAM	May worry too much about positive and negative events. May not assert their own needs: instead may become resentful. May be uncomfortable with confrontation.
AS A LEADER	Provides clear targets with a consideration for what others like to do. Establishes a clear structure with defined roles and responsibilities. Prefer a democratic leadership style using concrete facts and data.
WORKS BEST WITH	A relatively stable supportive environment. An opportunity to plan, prepare and have ample private time for regeneration.
WORKS LEAST WELL WITH/WHEN	Highly competitive, confrontational cultures. There is constant change and no positive feedback.

THEORISTS

TYPE	ENTJ: EXTRAVERTED MARSHALLER
DESCRIPTION	**Extraverted Marshallers** are direct, organized and possess a strong desire to make their inner visions a reality. They are quick thinking, strategic, logical decision-makers, possessing a drive for closure. They value intelligence or competence and abhor inefficiency. They conceptualize and theorize readily and possess the innate ability to take charge and make things happen. They exude confidence and appear energetic and driven. They are aware of intricate connections that they can explain with a logical model. As team members, they will want to ensure that the team is working efficiently to produce results, and may appear uncomfortable with too many emotional issues.
TEMPERAMENT	Theorist Need to be competent, knowledgeable and understand the universal operating principles in order to create their own destiny.
INTERACTION STYLE	In Charge Believe that it is worth taking a risk to decide and correcting later. Making rapid decisions to accomplish a clear future goal. Tend to appear quick moving, confident and determined.
DIRECTION OF ENERGY	Extraverting Energy goes outwards: process externally and tend to initiate interaction.
FIRST FUNCTION (ADULT)	Systematizing (Te) Making decisions using logical criteria to achieve goals by planning and organizing logistics and events in the external world. Adept at marshalling resources to achieve goals in the most expedient manner. Strong push for closure.
SECOND FUNCTION (PARENT)	Visioning (Ni) Gather information by creating their complete idea or future direction. Able to step back and assimilate data into a complete model.
SHADOW FUNCTION (CHILD)	Experiencing (Se) May observe and gather sensory data as a support to the future picture. May explore using the function-attitude in such activities as art, exercise or hobbies.

SHADOW FUNCTION (BALANCING)	Valuing (Fi) May consider their internal values and beliefs, but this decision will be subservient to logical criteria. When under stress, this function-attitude causes individuals to appear rigid in defending principles.
STRENGTHS ON A TEAM	Create an organized systematic approach to defining plans and outcomes. Decisive, clear, direct and assertive in their communication. Think in terms of systems and models to achieve an objective or solve a problem. Assemble resources and drive others to participate.
POTENTIAL CHALLENGES ON A TEAM	May be perceived as controlling as they push to achieve closure. May be direct and to the point, to the extent of being offensive. May appear oblivious cold, impersonal and somewhat oblivious to interpersonal interaction.
AS A LEADER	Sells long-term direction and ideas boldly to others. Thrive on building plans to achieve complex, long-term outcomes. Constantly drives to make decisions using their powerful directing presence.
WORKS BEST WITH	Committed people who deliver what they are asked for and will be assertive with their own needs. A culture that encourages independence and autonomy.
WORKS LEAST WELL WITH	Team members who appear overly emotional and unenthusiastic. A cautious culture where consensus decision making against established norms is encouraged.

TYPE	INTJ: INTROVERTED MARSHALLER
DESCRIPTION	**Introverted Marshallers** approach life with an independent-minded, long-term vision coming from their internal world of possibilities. While they develop abstract visions, they put concrete action plans in place to make their goals happen They can always offer a detached, objective perspective with the propensity for original thought as they see patterns in external events. With their ability to categorize data, they are confident in their ideas and their ability to achieve their goals. They can appear determined as they strive to achieve their high standards of performance. As team members, they may not reveal their inner emotions, but they can be strongly loyal to the team and can always be relied upon for a neutral independent opinion.

TEMPERAMENT	Theorist Need to be competent, knowledgeable and understand universal operating principles in order to create their own destiny.
INTERACTION STYLE	**Chart the Course** Like to think ahead and predict the goal. Envisioning a future and creating a systematic plan to achieve the goal. Tend to appear calm, intense and focused.
DIRECTION OF ENERGY	Introverting Energy goes inwards: tend to process and reflect, don't see all emotions.
FIRST FUNCTION (ADULT)	Visioning (Ni) Gather information by creating their complete idea or future direction. Gather data, step back to incubate and then are often able to suggest breakthrough approaches.
SECOND FUNCTION (PARENT)	Systematizing (Te) Making decisions using logical criteria to achieve goals by planning and organizing logistics and events in the external world. When their future picture is complete, adept at organizing resources to achieve the desired result.
SHADOW FUNCTION (CHILD)	Valuing (Fi) May consider their internal values and beliefs, but this decision will be subservient to logical criteria. When internal values system is crossed, may appear rigid with views.
SHADOW FUNCTION (BALANCING)	Experiencing (Se) May observe and gather sensory data as a support to the future picture. When under stress they can become over absorbed in sensory data.
STRENGTHS ON A TEAM	Provide an innovative, independent and original perspective. Conceptual long-range thinkers with an ability to relate the parts to the overall big picture. Create general structures and devise strategies to achieve goals. Systems thinking using causal effect logic to organize and integrate ideas.
POTENTIAL CHALLENGES ON A TEAM	May become impatient with those who do not see their vision quickly enough. Can appear rigid with ideas and insist on having their own way. May become aloof and abrupt when trying to influence team members about their future picture.

AS A LEADER	Creates a challenging framework for the future. Develops people through coaching, although can be tough when necessary. Presenting a strategy with a focus on excellence and performance.
WORKS BEST WITH	An equal with other talented individuals. A high degree of autonomy and independence.
WORKS LEAST WELL WITH	A very flexible environment with individuals who need excessive positive feedback. A detail focused rule-based environment where there is no opportunity for independent decision making.

TYPE	ENTP: EXTRAVERTED INNOVATORS
DESCRIPTION	**Extraverted Innovators** are normally quick thinking, verbally expressive and focused on future opportunities. They thrive on looking at concepts and possibilities from multiple angles and then arguing their own philosophy or hypothesis. They are optimistic, gregarious and social. They enjoy debate and can be very persuasive. They naturally generate options and then are able to analyze them strategically, which makes them creative, abstract problem solvers. They are enterprising and resourceful; however they may have difficulty in the implementation of the idea. As team members they will be upbeat and enthusiastic, but their need to take centre stage and challenge other's viewpoints could wear down those around them.
TEMPERAMENT	Theorist Need to be competent, knowledgeable and understand universal operating principles in order to create their own destiny.
INTERACTION STYLE	Get Things Going Like to facilitate involvement from the group. Brainstorming possibilities to originate new models or points of view. Tend to appear expressive, up beat and casual.
DIRECTION OF ENERGY	Extraverting Energy goes outwards: process externally and tend to initiate interaction.
FIRST FUNCTION (ADULT)	Brainstorming (Ne) Constant external exploration of future possibilities, patterns and meanings. Reading between the lines and ability to look at situations from fresh new angles. Tendency to bounce ideas around.

SECOND FUNCTION (PARENT)	Analyzing (Ti) Make decisions using internal logical criteria and principles. Analyze how and why things work. Evaluate and sort against a mental model to achieve improvements. Possess a clear "point of view" which they are able to defend against differing perspectives.
SHADOW FUNCTION (CHILD)	Harmonizing (Fe) Will be aware of subjective criteria to optimize group interaction. May play the role of "social organizer."
SHADOW FUNCTION (BALANCING)	**Recalling (Si)** May go back to historic data to compare and contrast their possibilities with past experience. When under stress, may get stuck on what went wrong and project this into the future.
STRENGTHS ON A TEAM	Great at providing energy and thrust to new projects. Naturally optimistic and future focused. Rely on abstract data to infer solutions to problems – look at problems from a fresh perspective. Self confident and assertive, with an ability to argue both sides of an issue.
POTENTIAL CHALLENGES ON A TEAM	May talk too much to externally process ideas and possibilities: can benefit from learning to think before speaking. May not be able to track details as they overextend to explore multiple possibilities. May appear arrogant as they hold centre stage to present their viewpoint.
AS A LEADER	Believing that the impossible is within reach. Looking beyond the conventional solution and challenging team members to believe the impossible is achievable. Can be generous with praise, convincing in persuasion and careless of unnecessary bureaucracy.
WORKS BEST WITH	Bright people who are willing to try new things. With experts who need little day-to-day direction.
WORKS LEAST WELL WITH	A culture where there is lots of structure and a respect for the traditional ways of operating. A culture that requires excessive focus on detailed specific directions.

TYPE	INTP: INTROVERTED INNOVATORS
DESCRIPTION	**Introverted Innovators** spend their lives in a quest for logical purity and accuracy. Using abstract data from ideas, future possibilities, and meanings, they analyze this information to align with their internal models. They possess an insight into complex theories and constantly search for patterns and systems to internally categorize data. They often function autonomously as they absorb themselves in mastering and perfecting their theories. They possess a unique ability to dissect the complex and comprehend conceptual subtleties. They enjoy creating conceptual solutions but then may struggle with their implementation, as they live in their rich inner world. As team members, they may appear distanced from the "real world" and intense although they prove to be excellent strategists.
TEMPERAMENT	Theorist Need to be competent, knowledgeable and understand universal operating principles in order to create their own destiny.
INTERACTION STYLE	Behind the Scenes Like to take the time to reconcile many inputs. Analyzing and integrating multiple models to define new concepts. Tend to appear approachable, friendly and patient.
DIRECTION OF ENERGY	**Introverting** Energy goes inwards: tend to process and reflect, don't see all emotions.
FIRST FUNCTION (ADULT)	Analyzing (Ti) Make decisions using internal logical criteria and principles. Analyze how and why things work. Evaluate and sort against a mental model to improve the operation of the system. Ability to dissect arguments and data to assess validity and to come up with a completely different logical perspective.
SECOND FUNCTION (PARENT)	Brainstorming (Ne) Ability to explore future possibilities, patterns, and meanings and to read between the lines to what is occurring but not stated.
SHADOW FUNCTION (CHILD)	**Recalling (Si)** May go back to historic data, but may project negative past experiences into the future, particularly when competence is challenged.
SHADOW FUNCTION (BALANCING)	Harmonizing (Fe) Will be aware of subjective criteria to optimize group interaction and appear laid back and empathetic. Under stress, may be oblivious to what is appropriate for group interaction.

STRENGTHS ON A TEAM	Contribute an alternative, logical detached perspective. Use precision in communication – exactly the right and nuance for any given situation. Naturally create theoretical systems to explain how and why things work. Great researchers as they integrate new and complex data into their unique complex model.
POTENTIAL CHALLENGES ON A TEAM	May have no concept of external deliverables and time frames. May appear sceptical and overly analytical and struggle with practical implementation. May confuse others with overly long complex explanations.
AS A LEADER	Expects people to take responsibility for their own actions: lets team members define objectives and work towards achieving them independently. Constantly challenges the status quo: contributing quality, deliberate ideas. Tend to focus on abstract systems and models in diagnosing and understanding team performance.
WORKS BEST WITH	Consistent access to new projects which are cutting edge in their field. Freedom to explore how things work and to generate new ideas.
WORKS LEAST WELL WITH	Routine tasks which require detailed concrete application and tight deadlines. Non-expert team members and dealing with content and ideas that are being repeated and which might be viewed as redundant.

CATALYSTS

TYPE	ENFJ: EXTRAVERTED MENTORS
DESCRIPTION	Extraverted Mentors are outgoing, empathetic, expressive developers of people. They have a remarkable gift at seeing human potential and want to help others "be all that they can be." With their long-term focus, they like closure in their lives as they work to make their visions a reality. They are gifted communicators whether one-on-one, where they are able to get almost anyone to open up to them, or in front of a group, where they are able to stimulate a positive enthusiasm. They are highly attuned to the moods and emotions of those around them, and work to create a harmonious environment. As team members, they focus on meaningful communication in the team, and drive to create genuine interactions with their team members. However, their focus on achieving their vision could detract from wanting to achieve team harmony.
TEMPERAMENT	Catalyst Need to have a purpose and make a meaningful contribution to the greater good; helping people to develop.
INTERACTION STYLE	In Charge Likes to make expedient decisions. Moving forward quickly to achieve development goals for people. Tend to appear quick moving, confident and determined.
DIRECTION OF ENERGY	Extraverting Energy goes outwards: process externally and tend to initiate interaction.
FIRST FUNCTION (ADULT)	Harmonizing (Fe) Making decisions using subjective criteria to optimize group interaction. Sensitive to other people's wants and needs, with an ability to self-disclose to connect. When stressed may show emotions on their face.
SECOND FUNCTION (PARENT)	Visioning (Ni) Gather information by creating their own complete idea or future direction. Step back in order to assimilate data. Trust own intuitive insights.
SHADOW FUNCTION (CHILD)	Experiencing (Se) May observe and gather sensory data as a support to the future picture. May explore sensory activities in a more playful way: exercise, art, cooking, etc.

SHADOW FUNCTION (BALANCING)	Analyzing (Ti) May compare and contrast data against an internal model, but this will be superseded by appropriateness to the group. Under stress, may result in excessive questioning to clarify logic.
STRENGTHS ON A TEAM	Fluent verbal skills in uniting disparate views to achieve consensus. Create a positive safe communication climate with warmth and connections. Are adept at drawing out the ideas and thoughts of others to raise collaboration and team involvement. Seeing potential in others: they welcome the opportunity to develop others.
POTENTIAL CHALLENGES ON A TEAM	May neglect logical choices for decisions that will achieve group harmony. May need frequent positive feedback and become sensitive to what is perceived as criticism. May show emotions under stress.
AS A LEADER	Spots talent and is generous in encouraging it. Offers a future vision for the team insisting that people behave well with each other. Style is warm, inclusive and supportive.
WORKS BEST WITH	A culture where people support each other and there are strong individual relationships. A culture that is future focused and understands the importance of people.
WORKS LEAST WELL WITH	An environment where there is severe conflict or people seem cold. Loathes organizational politics and the unfairness that they represent.

TYPE	**INFJ: INTROVERTED MENTORS**
DESCRIPTION	**Introverted Mentors** are quietly insightful individuals who are constantly searching for deeper meanings and the coming into consciousness of their inner visions. They empathetically understand the feelings and motivations of others and are loyal to people and institutions. As tactful, thoughtful, and concerned individuals they demonstrate interest in the development of others. They are very private people; they quietly exert an influence over others. They use language that is full of imagery as they structure the external world to work towards their inner picture of the future. As team members they will be sensitive to their colleague's emotional issues on their constant quest to make their vision a reality. However, their drive to achieve their vision may not be tempered with reality.

TEMPERAMENT	Catalyst Need to have a purpose and make a meaningful contribution to the greater good: helping people to develop.
INTERACTION STYLE	**Chart the Course** Like to think ahead and predict the goal. Having insights on future potential and working with an individual to develop talent. Tend to appear calm, intense and focused.
DIRECTION OF ENERGY	**Introverting** Energy goes inwards: tend to process and reflect, don't see all emotions.
FIRST FUNCTION (ADULT)	Visioning (Ni) Gather information by creating their own complete idea of future direction. Need time to step back in order to assimilate data. Confident in suggesting innovative solutions.
SECOND FUNCTION (PARENT)	Harmonizing (Fe) Make decisions using subjective criteria to optimize group interaction. Sensitive to team dynamics and team members wants and needs.
SHADOW FUNCTION (CHILD)	Analyzing (Ti) May compare and contrast data against an internal model, but this will be superseded by appropriateness to the group.
SHADOW FUNCTION (BALANCING)	**Experiencing (Se)** May observe and gather sensory data as a support to the future picture, but they do not need to do so. When under stress may overload on sensory input.
STRENGTHS ON A TEAM	Creative, conceptual approach. Sensitive, compassionate and empathetic. Organized: good follow through skills. Integrate people and systems effortlessly.
POTENTIAL CHALLENGES ON A TEAM	Can be unclear in articulating their vision. May forget to apply reason to their insights. May become single-minded in pursuit of their vision and make arbitrary decisions.

AS A LEADER	Builds consensus through patient on-on-one discussions. Persistent in working towards their ideal outcome. Confident in their vision, they will encourage and support others in pursuit of the goal.
WORKS BEST WITH	Organizations which allow them to influence people in the longer term. An environment with a clear identity and purpose.
WORKS LEAST WELL WHEN	There are clashes between values and actual behaviour. Forced to carry out practical, detailed tasks within an impersonal culture.

TYPE	ENFP: EXTRAVERTED ADVOCATES
DESCRIPTION	**Extraverted Advocates** are energetic, spontaneous, warm-hearted individuals who constantly generate creative, ingenious options for the future. They see endless possibilities that relate to the people around them. They love abstract concepts and are able to see beyond the obvious to the hidden meanings and patterns. Their strong inner values guide their decision making, as they readily give appreciation and support to others. They are empathetic and engaging, keenly perceptive of others, and use their verbal fluency to persuade and influence those around them. As team members, they are enthusiastic and committed to the relationships that are important to them, although they sometimes may frustrate their colleagues with their lack of concrete focus and seemingly impractical ideas.
TEMPERAMENT	Catalyst Need to have a purpose and make a meaningful contribution to the greater good: helping people to develop.
INTERACTION STYLE	Get Things Going Like to facilitate involvement from the group. Brainstorming possibilities to advocate a cause and help people develop. Tend to appear expressive, up beat and casual.
DIRECTION OF ENERGY	**Extraverting** Energy goes outwards: process externally and tend to initiate interaction.
FIRST FUNCTION (ADULT)	Brainstorming (Ne) Constant external exploration of future possibilities, patterns, and meanings. Verbal discussion of possibilities. Ability to read between the lines to the hidden meaning below.

SECOND FUNCTION (PARENT)	Valuing (Fi) Makes decisions quietly, but firmly based on their own internal beliefs system. Guided by strong inner values and wish life to be in congruence with those. Will appear tolerant of differences until those values are crossed then they can appear rigid in those beliefs.
SHADOW FUNCTION (CHILD)	Systematizing (Te) Will make some decisions using logical criteria to plan and organize logistics & events in the external world. May play in this function organizing things like dinner parties.
SHADOW FUNCTION (BALANCING)	Recalling (Si) May go back to historic data, to compare and contrast. When under stress may project negative past experiences into the future. May see negative possibilities when none exist.
STRENGTHS ON A TEAM	Quick thinking and verbally expressive in exploring new ideas. Zest for life and enthusiasm for the cause, group or team. Act as a catalyst or crusader for new ideas. Generate creative possibilities.
POTENTIAL CHALLENGES ON A TEAM	May appear scattered as they take on multiple projects. May be reluctant to "close the door" on opportunities and therefore leave too many options open. May miss detailed implementation steps and fail to follow through on ideas.
AS A LEADER	Inspires belief in the impossible being possible and creates an open participative environment. Believes in the value of what each individual can contribute. Shares tasks on an informal collegiate basis versus a top down directing style.
WORKS BEST WITH	In an environment where creativity is supported. Where there is a human element in the culture.
WORKS LEAST WELL WITH/WHEN	There are many rules and a formalized logical structure for achieving results. An environment which has power struggles or where there are plans which could be seen to be adverse to people's interests.

TYPE	INFP: INTROVERTED ADVOCATES
DESCRIPTION	Introverted Advocates are quiet pursuers of their life's quest as they strive to live according to their strongly held internal values. Not wanting to take centre stage, they can appear reserved and somewhat aloof until their internal belief system is "bumped up against" when they can react strongly in its defence. With a moral commitment to the fundamental worth of unique identity, they celebrate individual differences and want a purpose beyond a pay check. They are adaptable, and enjoy opportunities to explore the complexities of human personality. They value relationships based on authenticity and true connection. However they may frustrate their team mates with their constant push to live life according to their own internal ideals.
TEMPERAMENT	Catalyst Need to have a purpose and make a meaningful contribution to the greater good: helping people to develop.
DIRECTION OF ENERGY	Introverting Energy goes inwards: tend to process and reflect, don't see all emotions.
FIRST FUNCTION (ADULT)	Valuing (Fi) Make decisions quietly, but firmly based on their own internal beliefs system. Guided by strong inner values and wish life to be in congruence with those. Tolerant of differences until external behaviour is not in alignment with internal values.
SECOND FUNCTION (PARENT)	Brainstorming (Ne) Enjoy external exploration of future possibilities, patterns, and meanings. Can read between the lines and identify themes.
SHADOW FUNCTION (CHILD)	Recalling (Si) Will review past experience as a support to generating alternative ideas. May project negative past experiences into the future.
SHADOW FUNCTION (GROUNDING)	Systematizing (Te) Will make some decisions using logical criteria to plan and organize logistics and events in the external world. When values are crossed, are able to articulate a logical argument for their viewpoint. When under stress may obsess about details and achieving structure.
STRENGTHS ON A TEAM	In-depth concentration and output when involved in a project. Loyal to other team members if they believe in the cause. Reflect and produce intuitive insights, particularly in written form. Can act as the conscience for the team.

POTENTIAL CHALLENGES ON A TEAM	May find it difficult to do what is perceived as "meaningless" work. May find it difficult to follow through on detailed implementation plans. May react strongly when values are crossed.
AS A LEADER	Encourages creativity and participation. Passionate about causes, values and ideals. Starts from a basis of "how we will behave" and provides praise to motivate.
WORKS BEST WITH	Where behaviour is in alignment with articulated values and beliefs. A flexible environment where they can work in burst of energy.
WORKS LEAST WELL WITH/WHERE	In an impersonal regimented environment. They have to interact with people all the time and there are tight rigid deadlines.

Appendix Two

Understanding Type Dynamics

TYPE AND HIERARCHY OF FUNCTIONS

Type	Improviser						
Hierarchy of Functions	**ISTP** **Chart the Course**		**ISFP** **Behind the Scenes**		**ESTP** **In Charge**		**ESFP** **Get Things Going**
1st – Adult	Ti	Analyzing	Fi	Valuing	Se	Experiencing	Se	Experiencing
2nd – Parent	Se	Experiencing	Se	Experiencing	Ti	Analyzing	Fi	Valuing
3rd – Child	Ni	Visioning	Ni	Visioning	Fe	Harmonizing	Te	Systematizing
4th – Balancing	Fe	Harmonizing	Te	Systematizing	Ni	Visioning	Ni	Visioning
5t – Opposing	Te	Systematizing	Fe	Harmonizing	Si	Recalling	Si	Recalling
6th – Critical Parent	Si	Recalling	Si	Recalling	Te	Systematizing	Fe	Harmonizing
7th – Trickster	Ne	Brainstorming	Ne	Brainstorming	Fi	Valuing	Ti	Analyzing
8th – Demonic	Fi	Valuing	Ti	Analyzing	Ne	Brainstorming	Ne	Brainstorming

Type Hierarchy of Functions	Stabilizer							
	ISTJ Chart the Course		ISFJ Behind the Scenes		ESTJ In Charge		ESFJ Get Things Going	
1st – Adult	Si	Recalling	Si	Recalling	Te	Systematizing	Fe	Harmonizing
2nd – Parent	Te	Systematizing	Fe	Harmonizing	Si	Recalling	Si	Recalling
3rd – Child	Fi	Valuing	Ti	Analyzing	Ne	Brainstorming	Ne	Brainstorming
4th – Balancing	Ne	Brainstorming	Ne	Brainstorming	Fi	Valuing	Ti	Analyzing
5t – Opposing	Se	Experiencing	Se	Experiencing	Ti	Analyzing	Fi	Valuing
6th – Critical Parent	Ti	Analyzing	Fi	Valuing	Se	Experiencing	Se	Experiencing
7th – Trickster	Fe	Harmonizing	Te	Systematizing	Ni	Visioning	Ni	Visioning
8th – Demonic	Ni	Visioning	Ni	Visioning	Fe	Harmonizing	Te	Systematizing

Type Hierarchy of Functions	Theorist							
	INTJ Chart the Course		INTP Behind the Scenes		ENTJ In Charge		ENTP Get Things Going	
1st – Adult	Ni	Visioning	Ti	Analyzing	Te	Systematizing	Ne	Brainstorming
2nd – Parent	Te	Systematizing	Ne	Brainstorming	Ni	Visioning	Ti	Analyzing
3rd – Child	Fi	Valuing	Si	Recalling	Se	Experiencing	Fe	Harmonizing
4th – Balancing	Se	Experiencing	Fe	Harmonizing	Fi	Valuing	Si	Recalling
5t – Opposing	Ne	Brainstorming	Te	Systematizing	Ti	Analyzing	Ni	Visioning
6th – Critical Parent	Ti	Analyzing	Ni	Visioning	Ne	Brainstorming	Te	Systematizing
7th – Trickster	Fe	Harmonizing	Se	Experiencing	Si	Recalling	Fi	Valuing
8th – Demonic	Si	Recalling	Fi	Valuing	Fe	Harmonizing	Se	Experiencing

Type	Catalyst							
Hierarchy of Functions	INFJ Chart the Course		INFP Behind the Scenes		ENFJ In Charge		ENFP Get Things Going	
1st - Adult	Ni	Visioning	Fi	Valuing	Fe	Harmonizing	Ne	Brainstorming
2nd - Parent	Fe	Harmonizing	Ne	Brainstorming	Ni	Visioning	Fi	Valuing
3rd - Child	Ti	Analyzing	Si	Recalling	Se	Experiencing	Te	Systematizing
4th - Balancing	Se	Experiencing	Te	Systematizing	Ti	Analyzing	Si	Recalling
5t - Opposing	Ne	Brainstorming	Fe	Harmonizing	Fi	Valuing	Ni	Visioning
6th - Critical Parent	Fi	Valuing	Ni	Visioning	Ne	Brainstorming	Fe	Harmonizing
7th - Trickster	Te	Systematizing	Se	Experiencing	Si	Recalling	Ti	Analyzing
8th - Demonic	Si	Recalling	Ti	Analyzing	Te	Systematizing	Se	Experiencing

Appendix Three

Resource Guide

CHAPTER TWO: MYERS-BRIGGS TYPE INDICATOR®

2. 1. For more specifics on Concrete and Abstract Language

Please refer to the *Teamwork from the Inside Out Field Book* pages 49-51. Davies Black publishing 2003. Susan Nash and Courtney Bolin.

2.2 Additional resources for type descriptions are as follows:

Mc Guinness, Mary *You've Got Personality* Institute for Type Development 2004

Berens, Linda. V., Nardi, Dario. *The 16 Personality Types: Descriptions for Self-Discovery.* Huntington Beach, California: Telos, 1999.

Berens, Linda. V. et al, *Quick Guide to Personality Types in Organizations.* Huntington Beach, California: Telos, 2002.

Briggs-Myers, Isabel An Introduction to Type: A Guide to Understanding Your Results on the Myers-Briggs Type Indicator: European English Version (Paperback) 2000

Brownsword, Alan W. *It Takes All Types.* Baytree Publication Company 1994

Krebs Hirsh, Sandra and Kummerow, Jean M. *Introduction to Type in Organizations:*

Individual Interpretive Guide (Paperback) Oxford Psychologists Press

Rogers, Jenny *Sixteen Personality Types at Work in Organizations* Management Futures 1997

Nash, Susan *Turning Team Performance Inside Out* Davies Black 1999

Nash, Susan *Dating, Mating and Relating* Oxford, UK: HowTo Books 2000

CHAPTER THREE: MULTIPLE LENSES OF TYPE

3.1. For more specifics on Function-Attitudes please refer to the following texts.

Nash, S. *Turning Team Performance Inside Out.* Palo Alto, CA: Davies-Black, 1999.

Nash, S. *Dating, Mating and Relating* Oxford, UK: HowTo Books 2000

Nash, S. and Bolin, C. *Teamwork from the Inside Out Field Book* Palo Alto, CA: Davies-Black, 2003

Thompson, Henry Dick Ph. D. *Jung's Function-Attitudes Explained* Wormhole Publishing, 1996

Hartzler, G. and Hartzler, M. *Facets of Type: Activities to Develop the Type Preferences* Telos Publications 2004

Hartzler, G. and Hartzler, M. *Functions of Type: Activities to Develop the Eight Jungian Functions* Telos Publications 2005

Nardi, Dario *8 Keys to Self Leadership* Unite Business Press 2005

Berens, Linda V. Ph.D and Nardi, Dario *Understanding Yourself and Others: An Introduction to the Personality Type Code* Telos Publications 2004

Myers, Katherine D. and Kirby, Linda K. *Introduction to Type Dynamics and Development* Consulting Psychologists Press 1994

Haas, Leona and Hunziker, Mark *Building Blocks of Personality Type* Unite Business Press 2006

3.2. For more specifics on Beebe's Archetypes model please refer to the following texts.

Harris, Anne Singer (1996). *Living With Paradox: An Introduction to Jungian Psychology*, (especially Chapters 4 and 5, pp. 39-85). Pacific Grove, CA: Brooks/Cole Publishing Co.

Jung, C. G. (1971). *Psychological Types* (R.F.C. Hull, trans.), Volume 6 of *The Collected Works of C. G. Jung,* (H. Read, M. Fordham, G. Adler, and W. McGuire, eds.) Princeton: Princeton University Press (especially Chapters X and XI, pp. 330-486).

Sharp, Daryl (1987). *Personality Type: Jung's Model of Typology*. Toronto: Inner City Books.

Spoto, Angelo (1995). *Jung's Typology in Perspective* (revised edition). Wilmette, IL: Chiron Publications.

Von Franz, Marie-Louise and Hillman, James (1984). *Lectures on Jung's Typology*. Dallas: Spring Publications.

Beebe, John (2004) *Understanding Consciousness Through the Theory of Psychological Types,* in J. Cambray & L. Carter, *Analytical Psychology*, Hove and New York: Brunner Routledge, pp 83-115.

Beebe, John (1992) *Integrity in Depth*, College. Station, Texas A & M University Press.

Jung, C.G. 1971 (1921), *Psychological Types* (The collected works of C G Jung, Volume 6), London: Routledge.

3.3. For more specifics on temperament please refer to the following texts.

Nash, S. *Turning Team Performance Inside Out*. Palo Alto, CA: Davies-Black, 1999.

Nash, S. *Dating, Mating and Relating* Oxford, UK: HowTo Books 2000

Nash, S. and Bolin, C *Teamwork from the Inside Out Field Book* Palo Alto, CA: Davies-Black, 2003

Berens, Linda. V. *Understanding Yourself and Others: An Introduction to Temperament-3.0.* Huntington Beach, California: Telos, 2000.

Berens, Linda. V. and Gerke, Susan K. *The I in Team* Huntington Beach, California: Telos, 2005.

Delunas, E. *Survival Games Personalities Play*. SunInk Publications, 1992.

Keirsey, D. *Please Understand Me II*. Del Mar, CA: Prometheus Nemesis Books, 1998.

Keirsey, D. Choiniere, R *Presidential Temperament* . Del Mar, CA: Prometheus Nemesis Books, 1992.

Keirsey, D. and Bates, M. *Please Understand Me*. Del Mar, CA: Prometheus Nemesis Books, 1978.

Tieger, P. D., and Barron-Tieger, B. *Do What You Are*. Boston: Little, Brown, 1995.

Tieger, P. D., and Barron-Tieger, B. Nurture by Nature: Little, Brown, 1997.

Also, please refer to the following web-based self discovery product Interstrength® CogBooks™. This web-based self discovery tool is the result of a partnership between Interstrength Associates, Huntington Beach, California and CogBooks, LTD, Edinburgh, Scotland. For more information contact Interstrength Associates, 714-841-0041. http://www.inter-strength.com/products/13

3.4. For more specifics on Interaction Style please refer to the following texts.

Berens, Linda. V. *Understanding Yourself and Others: An Introduction to Interaction Style -2.0*. Huntington Beach, California: Telos, 2008.

Berens, Linda. V. and Gerke, Susan K. *Quick Guide to Interaction Styles™ and Working Remotely*. Huntington Beach, California: Telos, 2003.

Gerke, Susan K. and West, Karon *Quick Guide to Interaction Styles™ and Time Dynamics*. Huntington Beach, California: Telos, 2003.

Berens, Linda. V. adapted from Brad Cooper *Groundbreaking Sales Skills®: Portable Sales Techniques to Ensure Success* . Huntington Beach, California: Telos, 2004.

Also, please refer to the following web-based self discovery product Interstrength® CogBooks™. This web-based self discovery tool is the result of a partnership between Interstrength Associates, Huntington Beach, California and CogBooks, LTD, Edinburgh, Scotland. For more information contact Interstrength Associates, 714-841-0041. http://www.inter-strength.com/products/13

3.5 For more specifics on Developmental Factors please refer to the following texts.

Nardi, Dario Ph. D. *Multiple Intelligences and Personality Type: Tools and Strategies for Developing Human Potential* Huntington Beach, CA: Telos Publications, 2001

Nardi, Dario Ph. D *Character and Personality Type: Discovering your Uniqueness for Career and Relationships Success*. Huntington Beach, CA: Telos Publications, 2000

3.6 Other General Recommended Texts around Type

Fitzgerald, C., and Kirby, L. K. *Developing Leaders*. Palo Alto, CA: Davies-Black, 1997.

Hirsh, S. *Work It Out: Clues for Solving People Problems at Work*. Palo Alto, CA: Davies-Black Publishing, 1996.

Hirsh, Sandra and Jean Kummerow. *Life Types*. New York: Warner Books, Inc., 1989.

Isachsen, O., and Berens, L. *Working Together*. San Juan Capistrano, CA: Institute for Management Development, 1988.

Myers, Isabel Briggs and Peter B. Myers. *Gifts Differing*. Palo Alto: Consulting Psychologists Press, Inc., 1980.

Nash S: *Starting and Running Your Own Consultancy* Business: Oxford UK: HowTo Books 2008

Quenk, Naomi. *Beside Ourselves*: *Our Hidden Personality in Everyday Life*: Davies Black Publishing. 1993.

Segal, Marci *Creativity and Personality Type*, Huntingdon Beach CA, Telos Publications 2001

Hirsh, Katherine W and Hirsh, Elizabeth *Introduction to Type and Decision Making* CPP 2007

Hirsh, Katherine W, Hirsh, Elizabeth and Hirsh, Sandra Krebs Hirsh *Introduction to Type and Teams* CPP 2003

Dunning, Donna *Introduction to Type and Communication* CPP 2003

Berens, Linda V., Ernst, Linda K., and Smith, Melissa A. *Quick Guide to the 16 Personality Types and Teams* Huntington Beach, California: Telos, 2004.

Killen, Damian and Murphy, Danice *Introduction to Type and Conflict* CPP 2003

Pearman, Roger R. *Introduction to Type and Emotional Intelligence* CPP 2002

Hirsh, Sandra K., and Kise, Jane A. *Introduction to Type and Coaching* CPP 2003

Killen, Damien, and Williams, Gareth *Introduction to Type and Innovation* CPP 2006

Richmond, Sharon Lebovitz, *Introduction to Type and Leadership* CPP 2008

About the Author

Susan Nash

Susan Nash is the British-born owner of EM-Power, Inc., and EM-Power (UK) Limited.

Established in 1994, **EM-Power** has provided customized consulting services and training programs to over 500 companies in the US and Europe. EM-Power believes that a successful business consulting company must understand its clients' business needs and drivers in order to deliver customized services and programs that provide specific business results. EM-Power helps customers to ensure that any learning and development solution is not just an event, but part of the journey to achieve their business goals.

EM-Power provides business consulting services in the following five areas:

Applying Type Lenses (MBTI®) in Business

Susan is an international expert in business applications of Type and Temperament and author of six books, including *Turning Team Performance Inside Out*, *Dating Mating and Relating* and *The Teamwork from the Inside Out Field Book*. She has worked with type and teams for more than 18 years, and has introduced more than 20,000 people to best-fit personality type. EM-Power Inc. is a certification provider for MBTI® in the US, and Susan, who is on the Faculty of Interstrength Associates, runs certification programs in Europe. Susan is a regular contributor to *APTi Bulletin of Psychological Type*, *TypeFace*, and the *Australian Psychological Type Review* on such subjects as coaching, team building, leadership and best-fit type. Susan offers a variety of workshops including "Coaching from the Inside Out," "Leading from the Inside Out" and "Behind the Four Letter Code" plus Train The Trainer Accreditation for Temperament and Interaction Style in Europe.

Managing the Customer Experience

EM-Power helps companies maximise the Customer Experience with their clients. Based on the model originally developed with British Airways and incorporating the Crosby Continuous Improvement Philosophy, EM-Power's process defines critical activities necessary to ensure consistent excellent service delivery in five specific areas and helps clients to implement service improvement strategies.

Consulting for Retail Success

EM-Power helps retail organizations improve their sales and performance by customizing sales training programs, developing managers' skill levels, and delivering motivational/awareness programs for line personnel. These programs can be delivered by EM-Power trainers, or by internal trainers following a Train the Trainer process, using a comprehensive Training Guide for each program.

Developing Performance Skills

EM-Power runs a complete range of skills building programs including: Management and Supervisory Skills (Evaluating Performance, Behavioral Interviewing, Coaching Skills and Objective Setting), Individual Development Skills (Time Management, Presentation Skills, Conflict Resolution and Managing Meetings) and Sales Skills (Sales Training, Telephone Sales, and Sales Presentation Skills).

Performance Coaching

The EM-POWER coaching process is designed to capitalize on an individual's innate strengths, overcome potential weaknesses to achieve specific business and career goals.

For further information please visit the website at **www.em-power.com** or **www.em-poweruk.com** or contact EM-Power directly:

9 Westwood Road, Marlow, Bucks SL 7 2AT, United Kingdom.
Phone: +44 (0) 1628 891481
Susan.nash@em-power.com

AUG 1 8 2010

9 780956 327901